SPIRAL GUIDE

£9.99
C80

GW00419194

JRKISH
COAST

AA
Publishing

Contents

the magazine 5

Finding Your Feet 27

Istanbul and the Western Black Sea Coast 37

North Aegean 61

South Aegean 79

Written by Lindsay Bennett
Where to Stay and Where to Eat and Drink sections by Kevin Gould
Page layout by Dennis Buckley

Updated by Lindsay Bennett
Update managed by Bookwork Creative Associates

Published by AA Publishing, a trading name of Automobile
Association Developments Limited, whose registered office is Fanum
House, Basing View, Basingstoke, Hampshire RG21 4EA.
Registered number 1878835.

ISBN-13: 978-0-7495-3561-2

The contents of this publication are believed correct at the time of
printing. Nevertheless, AA Publishing accept no responsibility for
errors, omissions or changes in the details given, or for the conse-
quences of readers' reliance on this information. This does not
affect your statutory rights. Assessments of the attractions, hotels
and restaurants are based upon the author's own experience and
contain subjective opinions that may not reflect the publisher's opin-
ion or a reader's experience. We have tried to ensure accuracy, but
things do change, so please let us know if you have any comments or
corrections.

A CIP catalogue record for this book is available from the
British Library.

Reprinted 2008. Information verified and updated.
© Automobile Association Developments Limited 2003, 2005,
2008
Maps © Automobile Association Developments Limited 2003,
2005, 2008

Cover design and binding style by permission of AA Publishing
Colour separation by Leo Reprographics
Printed and bound in China by Leo Paper Products

Find out more about AA Publishing and the wide range of services
the AA provides by visiting our website at www.theAA.com/travel.

A03439

the magazine

It might be a cliché but East really does meet West in Turkey, both socially and geographically. But while this 80-year-old republic still represents the unique melding of Eastern and Western cultures, it's also willing to strike out for itself in search of future security and prosperity.

east

The Centre of the World

Turkey sits astride two continents, its land crossing the frontiers of Europe and Asia. Rubbing shoulders with the European Union in the west, it borders the recently troubled Balkan states to the northwest and fledgling post-Soviet republics to the north, but is also closely linked with the Middle East by its borders with Iran and Iraq in the east, and is only a stone's throw from Israel and the oil-rich states to the southeast.

The Cradle of Civilisation

Turkey has always been a buffer between enemies and a bridge between friends. Throughout history this land was coveted for its strategic importance by all the cultures coming west by sea or overland from the east. It was the battleground first between the ancient Greeks and the Persians, and later, during the more stable Roman and Byzantine Empires, it was the western terminus of the overland Silk

Top: A meeting of minds at Hierapolis's ancient theatre

Above: Detail of a carved window at İlyas Bey Camii at Milet (Miletos)

Previous page: Istanbul's thronging Mahmut Paşa market

Left: Designer goods are on sale in many Turkish bazaars

meets

WEST

Road, the source of luxury goods from China and India.

The Focus of Religion
Whoever controlled the capital on the banks of the Bosphorus influenced most of the known world. The glittering city of Constantinople was regarded as God's seat on earth and was the most important Christian centre until the mid-15th century, when the mighty Ottomans (► 17) converted the churches into mosques.

Renamed Istanbul, the city was at the heart of the Ottoman Empire which stretched into the Middle East and around the Mediterranean.

The Leader of the Pack
The new republic, created in the 1920s, was keen to pave the way for a more Western-style society. Modern Turkey is the only country to have adopted a fully secular constitution after having been an Islamic state (► 14–15), and

EAST meets WEST

one of few secular republics with a majority Muslim population. The country joined NATO in 1952 and the huge US air force base at Eçevit has been used in political situations. Turkey is a founder member and leading force in the Black Sea Economic Co-operation Group, whose affiliates include Armenia, Georgia, Azerbaijan, Moldova, Ukraine, Albania, Bulgaria, Greece, Romania and the Russian Federation. This economic union has a collective population of more than 350 million people and the world's second-largest reserves of oil and natural gas.

The Question of Europe

However, although Turkey sits apart from its Asian Islamic neighbours, it isn't fully integrated with Western economies either. Turkey is keen to become a member of the European Union, but has seen the EU community grow to 25 countries as it has stood in the wings. Ankara was invited to enter the official bidding process by Brussels in 2005, however, the process is stalled as some governments including the new Sarkozy regime in France, a major beneficiary of the current Common Agricultural Policy, raise concerns about integration of this large, mainly agrarian society. This adds to fears in Turkey itself that the application may be sidelined for years, with untold effects on the country's economic and political life.

The Faithful
People of a
Secular State

You'll know that you've truly relaxed in Turkey when the cadence of the early morning Islamic call to prayer (the *ezan*) becomes part of the melody of the night rather than a jolting interruption to a restful sleep. More than 90 per cent of Turkey's population is Muslim, and for most visitors the lilting reedy sound of the *ezan* is the most obvious sign of Islam's significance.

But unlike its neighbours to the east, where more fundamentalist Muslim societies live within the strict framework of *Sharia* or *Shari'ah* (Islamic religious law), Turkey is a secular nation where religion and state politics are separate. Faith is regarded as a personal matter, and many Turks live by Islam's major tenets but are more relaxed about the minor ones.

Right: The slender minarets of Sultanahmet Camii in Istanbul

Inset: Muslim men must perform ritual ablutions before entering the mosque

The Influence of Islam

The youngest of the world's major religions, Islam is the worship of Allah and reverence for his prophet, Mohammed. The word "Islam" means "surrender", and Muslims are those who have surrendered to Allah's will, accepting him as the one true God from whom all things come.

The sermons of Mohammed (born cAD 570) were written in the Koran, the holy book of Islam, which Muslims believe

Mosque Etiquette
- Women should cover their head and shoulders and men should wear long trousers.
- Shoes should be removed.
- Non-Muslims should not visit during prayer time.
- Do not photograph men at prayer.
- Respect the mosque as a holy space and don't make too much noise.

to be the true word of God. The *Sunna* (tradition), a collection of stories (*hadith*) about the life of Mohammed and his close followers, offers practical applications of the Koran's more obscure chapters. Together, these texts developed into *Sharia*. Sharia law, which has changed little since it was formulated between the 6th and the 9th centuries, covers every aspect of life from politics, law and education to family life, dress and diet and is still the basis of government in many Muslim countries.

Radical Reforms

Until the foundation of the Turkish Republic in 1923, Turkish law was based on Sharia law. However, the new president, Mustafa Kemal (► 14–15) saw this as being key to Turkey's failure to keep up with technological and industrial advances in Europe and America. His radical new constitution introduced secular law and education systems, as well as policies for economic development. In a series of dramatic reforms, he sought to extinguish what he regarded as backward-looking religious influence completely, even banning the Arabic *ezan* during the 1930s.

To many Turkish people, this was a step too far. While they were happy to embrace capitalism and secular law, they still put their faith resolutely in Allah. Although a powerful cult of personality stifled all opposition during Atatürk's lifetime, less than 20 years after his death a "populist" government reinstated the *ezan*, among other things, in an attempt to redress the balance and place faith back into the hands of the people.

Modern Turkey

Today, Islam coexists with the modern republic, and Turkish society displays a fascinating blend of religious viewpoints from the agnostic to the devout. You'll find Turks enjoying activities that are usually forbidden in Islamic countries: men drinking alcohol, urban women dressed in the latest European fashions and Lotto ticket vendors demonstrating Turks' love of games of chance. But, you'll also see modestly dressed professional women with their heads covered by a scarf and trendy youths gathering at a mosque for Friday prayers .In a region beset by sectarian violence, Turks continue to find balance between personal faith and the secular state.

Right: A moment of prayer in Istanbul's Sultanahmet Camii

The Five Pillars of Islam

The Koran lays down five obligations for all Muslims:

- The profession of faith
- Prayer five times a day
- Fasting during the holy month of Ramadan (Ramazan in Turkish) except for pregnant women, the elderly, the sick, travellers and young children
- Charity to the poor
- At least one pilgrimage to the Kaaba in Mecca (the most holy site in Islam)

Best Beaches
- **Ölüdeniz** (▶ 114–115): some say it's been over-developed, but it's still a picture-perfect beach protecting a languid lagoon.
- **Patara** (▶ 123): A protected 20km (12-mile) stretch of sand shared only with nesting turtles.
- **Olympos** (right, ▶ 162–163): sheltered from the world by high, pine-clad ridges.

Best Historical Buildings
- **Ephesus** (left, ▶ 84–87): the most complete ancient city in the eastern Mediterranean.
- **Aya Sofya Camii** (▶ 42–43) in Istanbul: God's seat on earth in the Byzantine era.
- **Cappadocia** (▶ 149–150): ornate Byzantine churches carved into soft volcanic rock.
- The **citadel at Alanya** (▶ 144–145): more than 7km (4 miles) of crenellated walls perched on a rocky outcrop.
- The **Petronium at Bodrum** (▶ 94–95): a crusader castle now home to the Museum of Underwater Archaeology.

Best Boat Trips
- Touring the waters off **Kekova Adası** (Kekova Island, ▶ 116–117), with its secluded coves and a sunken city just below the waterline.
- **Dalyan** (▶ 112–113) offers something for everyone: freshwater lakes and reed beds, a fantastic beach with nesting turtles, mud baths and ancient remains.

Best Bazaar
Istanbul's 650-year old **Kapalıçarşı** (Grand Bazaar, ▶ 49–50), the world's original shopping mall, still filled with treasures.

Most Exhilarating Activities

- Rafting on the **Köprülü River** (above, ▶ 140–141).
- **Tandem paraglide** from Mount Baba above Ölüdeniz (▶ 122): said to be the biggest vertical drop by parasail in the world.

Most Striking Landscapes
- Pine-covered mountain ranges beyond **Antalya** (▶ 134).
- "Fairy chimneys": eroded tufa columns in **Cappadocia** (▶ 149–150).
- Cliffs sweeping down to azure waters near **Kaş** on the Turquoise coast (▶ 123).

Best Natural Moments
- **Olympos Milliparkı** (Olympos Beydağları National Park, ▶ 162–163) with its extensive forest and walking trails.
- **Dilek Yarımadası/Büyük Menderes Deltesi Milliparkı**, ▶ 97–98) offers the remote chance of seeing an Anatolian leopard.

The Best of the Turkish Coast

Most Photogenic Views
• From the temple mount at **Assos** (➤ 73–74)
• Down Curetes Street at **Ephesuş** (➤ 84–87)
• From the citadel at **Alanya** (➤ 144–145)
• The town of **Simena** from Kekova sound (➤ 116–117)

If you only see two...
...**statues**, make them the majestic **Artemis** in the Museum at Selçuk (➤ 88) and the **Medusa** at Didyma (below, ➤ 100–101)
...**sunsets**, look across the waters of **Lake Bafa** (➤ 159–161), and over the travertine pools at **Pamukkale** (➤ 92–93)

If you only go to one...
...**nightclub**, make it Disco Halikarnas in Bodrum (➤ 95)

"There are two Mustafa Kemals. One the flesh and blood Mustafa Kemal...the other is you...I stand for the nation's dreams, and my life's work is to make them come true."

Atatürk

Father of Modern Turkey

You can't fail to notice his steely countenance on Turkish bank notes and in the statues gracing every town square, but who was Mustafa Kemal, the man who became known as Atatürk – Father of the Turks?

The founder and first president of the Turkish Republic, Kemal is still admired and respected by the Turkish people.

Born simply Mustafa in 1881, he was given the name Kemal, which means "perfection", while at the Ottoman military academy. This drive towards achievement defined everything he did, from

Left: An equestrian statue of Atatürk in Fethiye

leading the forces fighting the Turkish War of Independence to seeing his vision of Turkey take shape less than a decade later (▶ 10).

Kemal was interested in European philosophy, especially in the new "science" of sociology. Auguste Comte's (1798–1857) theory of Positivism was particularly influential; the belief that human beings were the masters of a world that could be explained in a scientific manner and controlled through logic and planned social structures. Positivism helped to shape Kemal as a political realist and he was never one to avoid making difficult decisions. One of the most significant was his approval of the unprecedented exchange of populations with Greece in the 1920s. In an attempt to prevent future racial tension, half a million Muslims were sent from Greece to Turkey, and 1.3 million Christians were sent from Turkey to Greece, leaving homes their families had known for generations.

But although he was renowned for his political astuteness, he seemed incapable of applying the same principles to himself. Exasperated by an apparent only attempt at a stable domestic life.

Alcohol was his only long-term companion, a disastrous relationship that began during his days as a junior officer and gradually fogged his judgement until he eventually died from cirrhosis of the liver in 1938 at the age of 57.

Above: Atatürk's tomb in the Turkish capital, Ankara
Right: Atatürk the statesman taken in later life

lack of progress, he became paralysed by bouts of depression. There were few friends with whom he could relax, and a short-lived marriage in the mid-1920s was his

Atatürk's Curriculum Vitae

Early career: 1905–23
- Rose through the Ottoman army to the rank of general.
- Hero at the Battle of Gallipoli (1915).
- Led popular insurrection against the Ottoman Sultanate (1921).

The presidential years: 1923–38
- Moulded a new constitution.
- Moved the capital from Istanbul to Ankara.
- Replaced Arabic with a new written and spoken Turkish language.
- Constructed a secular parliamentary and law system (► 10).
- Introduced metric measurement.
- Supplanted the Islamic lunar calendar with the Gregorian (Western) version.
- Decreed that education should be a universal right.
- Legislated for women's rights.
- Legitimised civil marriage and divorce.
- Criminalised polygamy.

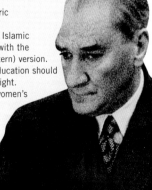

A QUICK HISTORY
of the
TURKISH COAST

3000BC–AD330

ANCIENT ASIA MINOR

3000 BC: Troy (► 74) is founded, to become the longest established city along the Turkish coast.

1200BC: Phrygians (from Europe) and Achaeans (from Greece) establish settlements on the west coast including Ephesus (► 84–87), Priene (► 98–99) and Miletos (► 99–100). Meanwhile, Pamphylians (from Southern Asia Minor) claim the Mediterranean coast and establish Perge (► 136–137), Side (► 142–143) and Aspendos (► 138–139).

1100BC: Dorians (early Greeks) and Ionians (from Greece) take the Phrygian cities, the seeds of a "Greek" population that would thrive in Turkey until the 1920s.

900–700BC:
other groups rise to prominence:
Lydians (from Western Asia Minor) in the
Northern Aegean establish Sardis (► 66–67);
Lycians along the Turquoise Coast establish
Myra (► 118–119), Fethiye (► 121) and
Kaunos (► 112–113); and the Carians are
centred on Bodrum (► 94–96) in the
Southern Aegean.

Above: Frieze detail from a Lycian rock tomb in Myra

Below: Alexander the Great

546BC: Persians invade from the east, ruling for
more than 200 years before being repelled by
Alexander the Great (334–329BC).

133BC: Western Turkey becomes part of the
Roman province of Asia Minor, with its early
capital at Pergamum (► 68), and relative peace
lasts for more than 400 years.

AD330–1453

THE BYZANTINE ERA

AD330: Emperor Constantine decrees that
Christianity is the one religion of the Roman state
and establishes a new capital, Constantinople, at
the tiny settlement of Byzantium, thereby founding
the Byzantine Empire.

c1000: Byzantium declines in influence as the first
millennium ends and Seljuk Muslims seize territory
along the south and west coasts, building among other
monuments, the citadel at Alanya (▶ 144–145).

1453–1922

THE OTTOMAN EMPIRE

1453: Constantinople is taken by Islamic Ottoman
forces, becoming their capital – Istanbul.

1560s: the Ottoman Empire experiences a golden age during the
reign of Süleyman the Magnificent and is at the zenith of its power.
Istanbul is a showpiece of Islamic architecture.

1600s: the Empire starts to decline.

1918–23: the Ottoman Empire ends in defeat after
World War I and Greece is given control of part of
Turkey's west coast, prompting an armed insurrection led
by Ottoman General Mustafa Kemal.

1923–present

THE TURKISH REPUBLIC

1923: Turkish Republic is founded. Its
first president, Mustafa Kemal
(▶ 14–15), oversees a population
exchange with Greece and a transforma-
tion of the country.

**Left: Atatürk
introduces
language
reforms into
the new
Turkish
Republic**

1938: death of Mustafa Kemal (Atatürk).

1974: Turkey invades Cyprus in response to an attempted
Greek coup on the island.

1980s and early 1990s: a boom in tourism leads
to massive development in the coastal resorts.

**Below: Antalya,
one of the
resorts to
experience the
tourist boom**

Late 1990s: the Turkish economy is in trouble as
the result of political instability, corruption and
financial mismanagement.

2005: Turkey devalues and restructures its
currency. Turkey is invited by Brussels to submit
an application to join the European Union.

2007: Abdullah Gül becomes the first Turk with
an Islamic background to become President since
the establishment of the Republic in 1923.

Tea and *tavla*

A young boy of about eight sits on a chair, an empty, round tin tray placed solidly on his lap, held there by folded arms. Always alert for the need of his services, he is closely observing the group of men huddled around the nearby table, and is excited by the clattering of dice and the boisterous verbal sparring of the group. A nod of an adult head sends him dashing to the kitchen to fill his tray with hot, clear tea in diminutive tulip-shaped glasses. On his return, he carefully distributes one to each player and the little spectator takes his front row position once more.

This is a daily ritual at his father's café, and, in fact, all across Turkey. In a land where relaxation is taken seriously, and a man's place is definitely not in the home, the tea shop is of vital

Let's Take Tea
• **Şark Kahvesi** in Istanbul's Kapalıçarşı (Grand Bazaar, ► 49–50) for city bustle
• **Kutes Kafetyria** in Kuşadası (► 97), for the company of fashionable Turks
• **Çeri Café** at Lake Bafa (► 161) where you'll probably find some peace

importance and games of backgammon – or *tavla* as it is known – offer the chance for men to socialise, think and pass a few hours. The theatrical throw of the dice and the audience that forms the coterie of tactical advisors are all part of the ritual.

In the countryside, after a hard morning's work, a farmer makes his way to the village café to while away the hot afternoon. He pulls up a chair to discuss the day's activities with his neighbours, to debate politics and to complain about the price of fuel for his farm machinery, all over a game of *tavla* and several cups of tea.

In towns, the café goes out to the men rather than vice-versa. For shopkeepers ensconced on the porches of their stores *tavla* games can last all day. The café owner

A Woman's Place

Although Turkish women do not tend to visit tea and coffee shops, foreign women, particularly in the countryside, will be made welcome and often found a place of honour, becoming in some senses an "honorary" man for the occasion.

sends out trays of tea to his neighbours in the surrounding streets, collecting the empties later on, confident that each man will pay for what he has drunk.

Tea delivery can earn a boy a few lira and, after school or in the holidays, sons or nephews serve a hard apprenticeship, striding deftly through the crowds with packed trays, rarely spilling a drop.

Below: Young men in Kaş engrossed in a game of *tavla*

Tea Talk

• Turkey produced over 205,000 tonnes of tea in 2005, a huge increase on pre-2000 figures. The main tea producing area is along the northeastern Black Sea coast.

• Tea shrubs can be pruned after 5 years and can give annual crops until they reach the age of 70.

• On average, everyone in Turkey drinks 2.5kg (5.5lb) of tea per year.

The Real Way to *Relax*

*I*n the grind of modern living we all want to relax. The Turks have the right idea: they've been taking regular water and massage treatments for centuries. Communal bathing in a steamy *hamam* (Turkish bath) has long been a part of Turkish life, catering for everyone, whether they are rich or poor. Lose your inhibitions and your stress by experiencing the pleasures of the *hamam* for yourself.

His and Hers

Hamams usually have separate sections for men and women, or are open at separate times for each sex, because Islam preaches modesty in relations between adult men and women. However, the advent of tourism has led to *hamams* in most resorts offering unisex sessions, so if you're part of a mixed couple or group, you can enjoy the experience together.

Prepare...

Most traditional *hamams* are found in the narrow alleys of a town's old quarter, behind an unpretentious, plain wooden door. When you enter you'll be given a *peştamal* (small robe; you can wear a swimsuit too if you feel more comfortable) and *takunya* (wooden clogs) or plastic sandals.

Wash...

Once changed, enter the inner sanctum, the *hararet* (steam chamber) where you'll be enveloped in hot, moist

air. First, wash thoroughly all over at one of the basins, then rinse yourself off with the water scoops provided – but don't get suds in the water. It's often used for Islamic ritual ablutions (washing before visiting the mosque) and shouldn't be contaminated.

Steam...

Next, prostrate yourself on the hot central marble slab, the *göbek taşı* (navel stone) for 15 or 20 minutes, allow-

The Perfect Rubdown

- **Çemberlitaş** in Istanbul (right, ► 157) – built during the reign of Süleyman the Magnificent, with separate sections for men and women
- **Kaleiçi Hamam** (Eylül Sokak No 7, Kuşadası, ► 97) – frequented by just about every European nationality. You'll find it next to the mosque and behind the post office
- **Fethiye Hamam** (Hamam Sokak No 2, Paspatur Bazaar) – a tiny 16th-century establishment in Fethiye (► 121).
- Enjoy a *haman* mid-way through your holiday and it will prolong your tan.

ing the heat to penetrate your pores.

Massage...

Now you're primed for the *tellak* (masseur), who will soap you up and rub you down with a *kese* (horse-hair flannel) for a startlingly thorough exfoliation. Then your flesh will be kneaded and your limbs manipulated to loosen tight muscles and joints – *tellaks* work according to the "no pain, no gain" principle so be warned!

...and Relax

After your treatment, wash yourself down, wrap yourself in towels and retire to the relaxation area to rest. You'll emerge feeling clean, glowing and refreshed. What could be better after a long day's sightseeing?

Let's Party!

As a bride's wedding day beckons, female family and friends join her at the *hamam* to eat snacks, tell stories and dispense advice while she is ritually cleansed and depilated – a hen night in all but name.

Left: The *hararet* or steam room, the heart of every Turkish *hamam*

Below left: A *tellak* (masseur) soaps up a client before her massage

According to legend, when the Ottoman forces crossed over on to European soil in 1453, they held a celebratory wrestling contest in which more than 40 competitors died rather than submit, so strong was their will to win. They might not be as single-minded today, but Turkish men still tend to spar with their friends and admire their sporting heroes, viewing trials of strength and friendly competition as a positive part of life.

Fanatical Followers

Right: Football is particularly popular in Turkey and there are several newspapers devoted to the sport

Dirty Tricks

Grease wrestling has always been the "king" of Turkish sports, though it's actually olive oil, not grease, that is applied to the body. It was discovered that olive oil on the skin could be used as a mosquito repellent when taking part in open-air sports and it became a tradition for competitors to douse themselves in oil. It's not just an excuse for greasy grappling, however: historically wrestlers were trained in the

Football Crazy

Only football generates bigger pay packets and more sporting attention than grease wrestling. In the last five years, Turkish clubs have increased their profile, winning several important European tournaments and inducing a football frenzy. The major clubs – Galatasaray, Fenerbahçe and Beşiktaş – are all based in Istanbul so only a few fanatical fans can actually get to see their matches. Newspapers, several devoted to this one sport alone, are avidly read for day-to-day information. But television is the major way of watching a match – if you happen to be eating at a restaurant when there's an important game on, forget about speedy and attentive service; all eyes will be on the screen in the corner and if the correct team scores, prepare for exuberant celebrations.

Below left: Jubilant Turkish football fans celebrate their team's success
Below: Grease wrestlers fight it out

tekkes (religious monasteries) of the Dervish order, imbuing the sport with a spiritual as well as a physical component,

Fast Track

In 2005, Istanbul became a big player in motor racing, holding the first Formula 1 Grand Prix at its bespoke Hermann Tilke designed track just outside Istanbul. The current lap record is held by Juan Pablo Montoya who covered the 5.344km (3.340-mile) circuit in just 1 minute 24.77 seconds.

similar to that in martial arts. Today, the prize money runs at more than $1,000,000 per year.

It takes around 20 years for turtles to mature. They return to land only to seek out their own birthplaces to lay their eggs. But the hatchlings that fought their way up through the sand of deserted Turkish beaches in the late 1970s returned to a different land-scape in the new millennium.

The Green

Left: A single turtle hatchling makes it to the open sea

Below: İstuzu Beach, an important turtle nesting site

Turkey was totally unprepared for the sudden explosion in visitor numbers in the 1980s and 1990s. There were no consistent strategies or regulated building plans and environmental concerns could not compete with the lure of the tourist lira. Tranquil fishing villages rapidly swelled into massive resorts and swathes of coastline disappeared under concrete and breeze block. Turtles faced not silent moonlit nesting sites but the blinding iridescent lights of hotels and thudding music from seafront bars, and their numbers plummeted.

Shelling Out

Ironically, as foreign income continued to increase during the early 1980s, the Ministry of Culture promoted natural attractions as one of Turkey's major assets. It was less eager, however, to defend these very attractions from development. It wasn't until the late 1980s that attitudes were forced to change. When a luxury resort complex was set to envelop İstuzu Beach, an important

Turtle Tableau

The Turkish coast has populations of both *Caretta caretta* (loggerhead) and *Chelonia mydas* (green) turtles (below). They have a lifespan of up to 70 years and mature females nest every other year, laying three or four clutches of up to 120 eggs, which take around two months to hatch. The newborns head straight out to sea, after which their behaviour is unknown – a period called "the lost years" by scientists.

National park staff run ticket booths rather than operating protective patrols and the only indications of "special" status are a few information boards set at intervals along the beach.

Conundrum

turtle-nesting site (▶ 113), opposition from foreign biologists and celebrities was intense. A wave of "turtle mania" spread among the very people Turkey hoped to attract – ordinary visitors. İstuzu was saved, along with 16 other nesting beaches designated sites of Special Environmental Protection.

A giant statue of two turtles in the main square in the nearby town of Dalyan commemorates the success of the campaign but İstuzu still typifies Turkey's green conundrum. Although throughout the nesting season (May to September) it's off-limits after dark, daylight brings hoardes of day-trippers, all anxious to catch a glimpse of a turtle, who trample unfettered across the sand – and perhaps across the developing eggs as well.

Looking to the Future

With its dramatic landscapes and rare wildlife, Turkey definitely has the raw material to take advantage of the growing ecotourism market. But the situation at İstuzu shows that it's still wrestling with a fundamental issue – defining an integrated and sustainable long-term strategy. In 20 years, perhaps the next generation of breeding turtles will have an easier time than their parents did.

Active Relaxation

Runner Tourism, Varlik Mah. Pirireis Cad 177, Sokak 5/1, 07050 Antalya (tel: 0252 237 9842, fax: 0242 237 9862; www.runnertourism.com) organise outdoor and eco-friendly holidays.

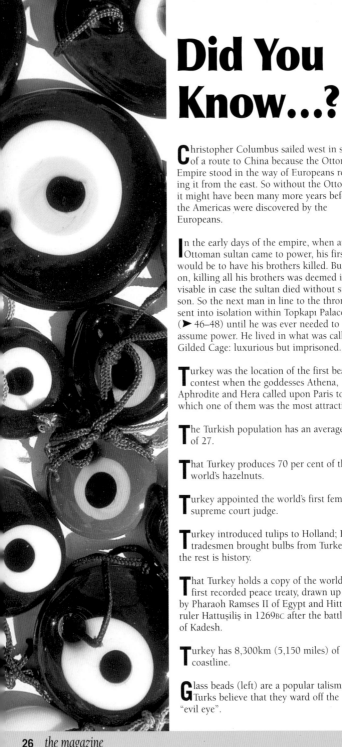

Did You Know...?

Christopher Columbus sailed west in search of a route to China because the Ottoman Empire stood in the way of Europeans reaching it from the east. So without the Ottomans, it might have been many more years before the Americas were discovered by the Europeans.

In the early days of the empire, when an Ottoman sultan came to power, his first job would be to have his brothers killed. But later on, killing all his brothers was deemed inadvisable in case the sultan died without siring a son. So the next man in line to the throne was sent into isolation within Topkapı Palace (➤ 46–48) until he was ever needed to assume power. He lived in what was called the Gilded Cage: luxurious but imprisoned.

Turkey was the location of the first beauty contest when the goddesses Athena, Aphrodite and Hera called upon Paris to judge which one of them was the most attractive.

The Turkish population has an average age of 27.

That Turkey produces 70 per cent of the world's hazelnuts.

Turkey appointed the world's first female supreme court judge.

Turkey introduced tulips to Holland; Dutch tradesmen brought bulbs from Turkey and the rest is history.

That Turkey holds a copy of the world's first recorded peace treaty, drawn up by Pharaoh Ramses II of Egypt and Hittite ruler Hattuşiliş in 1269BC after the battle of Kadesh.

Turkey has 8,300km (5,150 miles) of coastline.

Glass beads (left) are a popular talisman. Turks believe that they ward off the "evil eye".

Finding Your Feet

First Two Hours

The Turkish coast has several international airports, though most tend to handle charter flights rather than scheduled services. The exception is Istanbul's Atatürk Havalimanı (Atatürk Airport), which is also the hub for a network of onward domestic flights operated by Türk Hava Yolları (also known as THY or Turkish Airlines) and Istanbul Airlines.

Visas

- Those visitors to Turkey who require a tourist visa (► 170) can **purchase them on arrival in Turkey**, before going through passport control. Visas must be bought with **foreign currency**, preferably the currency of the passport holder, not Turkish lira. In sterling, visas currently cost £10 for which **only £10 notes are accepted.** No change is given.
- Tourist visas are **valid for three months** from the date of stamping.

Ground Transport Fees
£ under 5YTL   ££ 5–10YTL   £££ 10–15YTL   ££££ over 15YTL

Istanbul

- **Atatürk Airport** (www.ataturkairport.com) lies 25km (15.5 miles) west of Istanbul. The **arrivals terminal** contains a tourist information office, exchange services and car rental agencies.
- **Taxis** (££££) are the quickest and most direct method of reaching your hotel. You will find yellow taxis, marked "TAXI" or "TAKSI", outside the arrivals terminal. However, many **hotels offer a free pick-up service** from the airport – just let them know your flight number in advance. The journey into town takes about 40 minutes.
- **Havaş** runs **half-hourly bus services** (££) 4am–1am daily to THY offices on Cumhuriyet Caddesi, in the Taksim district. The journey takes around 60 minutes (longer at peak times). The Airport Express (£) route 96T runs from 5:40am–1:40am with services every five minutes at peak times. The journey time is around 60 minutes to Taksim, less to Eminönü.
- **Metro** services (£) take around 45 minutes with a terminus at Aksaray (www.istanbul-ulasim.com.tr).
- The **city centre tourist office** can be found at **Maydanı**, the Divan Yolu Caddesi end of the Hippodrome, in the Sultanahmet district.
- The historic heart of Istanbul is compact and you can walk between the main attractions. Taxis are inexpensive and plentiful. A north–south tram system (£, tickets from kiosks at each station) passes the Sultanahmet and the Bayoğlu/Taksim districts. Ferries link city districts that bound the water. From Sultanahmet the nearest ferry station is at Eminönü.

İzmir

- **Adnan Menderes Airport** (www.adnanmenderesairport.com) is situated 18km (11 miles) south of İzmir.
- Havaş operates a **shuttle bus** (££) between the airport and the THY office at the Büyük Efes Hotel in the city. Services run every 30 minutes between the first and last THY flights to arrive (from about 3am–11:30pm). Journey time is 45 minutes.
- The **Rapid Rail** service (£) will connect the airport to the city centre from April 2008. Services run 6am–11pm.

■ A **train service** (£) links the airport with the city's Alsancak station. It runs every half hour between 6am and 11pm, and takes just 20 minutes.

■ **Taxis** (£££; journey time: 30 minutes) are plentiful and depart from outside the terminal building.

■ The **city centre tourist office** is located at 1344 Sok 2, Pasaport district.

Bodrum

■ **Milas-Bodrum Airport** (www.bodrum-airport.com) is 35km (22 miles) east of Bodrum.

■ A **THY shuttle bus** (£), which awaits all THY flights, runs to the THY office in Bodrum at Neyzen Tevfik Caddesi. The journey takes about an hour.

■ **Taxis** (£££; journey time: 40 minutes) are plentiful.

■ There are **tourist offices** at the airport and near the castle, at Barış Meydanı.

Dalaman

■ **Dalaman Airport** is 3km (2 miles) from Dalaman. Tourist information, banks and car rental offices open to meet all flights during the tourist season.

■ There are **no public transport links** but taxis are available to Dalaman (£; 5 minutes), Dalyan (££; 30 minutes) and Fethiye (£££; one hour).

Antalya

■ **Antalya International Airport** (www.aytport.com) is 8km (5 miles) east of the city.

■ Havaş runs **shuttle buses** (£) from the airport to the Havaş office at Cumhuriyet Caddesi, half an hour away, after each THY flight.

■ **Taxis** (£) are numerous. It takes 20 minutes to get into town.

■ **Bus service** (£) from city to domestic terminal hourly 8:15am–10pm.

■ There are **tourist information offices** at the airport and in Cumhuriyet Caddesi, Özel İdare Altı 2, Kaleiçi.

Getting Around

Travelling along the Turkish coast can be time-consuming and, although the national bus service is excellent, it may be quicker to fly to regional airports. Many attractions can be visited by using local buses but others have no transport connections. The most flexible option for touring is a rental car.

Domestic Air Travel

■ Türk Hava Yolları (**THY** or Turkish Airlines) operates from Istanbul to the regional airports. Up to eight flights per day link Istanbul with İzmir, five with Antalya and one or more with Bodrum and Dalaman. THY may offer a discount on a domestic flight if you buy an international ticket.

Long-Distance Buses

■ Long-distance buses are frequent, reliable and comfortable. Price and quality do vary, but even at the luxury end of the market, the buses are relatively inexpensive.

■ Tickets should be bought in advance.

■ Numerous local companies contribute to the network but few mass-produce copies of their timetables. **Visit the *otogar*** (bus station) to compare prices and timetables, or find information and book tickets in advance from travel agencies. Don't take the word of the ticket touts.

■ All routes must take **rest stops** every 90 minutes. On longer journeys there is a 30-minute meal break. Journeys over ten hours take place at night.

Dolmuşes and Local Buses

- The *dolmuş* (shared car or minibus) system links towns with the suburbs, and resorts to outlying beaches and nearby tourist attractions. Services are inexpensive and reliable, departing when the *dolmuş* is full and dropping passengers anywhere along a set route. Services operate from about **7am–7pm**, but check for local and seasonal differences at station offices or on the timetable in the *dolmuş* itself.
- **Buses** link villages to major towns and depart to a set timetable, though remote villages may have only one or two services a day.
- There is **no advance ticket purchase**. Simply pay the driver or ticket boy on the bus or *dolmuş*.

Taxis

- Yellow taxis, marked on the doors or roof with a black "TAXI" or "TAKSI", are numerous. Though by far the most expensive form of transport, by international standards the fares are **good value**.
- You can hail a cab in the street or find a **taxi rank** – this is usually in a main square or on a principal thoroughfare.
- **All city taxis should have meters** but in country areas and coastal resorts it is accepted practice to agree a set price before travelling. Taxi drivers will negotiate hire of their cars for half a day or a full day.
- Fares **cost 50 per cent more** at night.

Car Rental

- To hire a car you'll need to have held a **full driving licence** for at least one year. Drivers should usually be over the age of 21 but some companies will only accept drivers over the age of 25.
- **Local car rental companies** offer lower prices than the international operators, but check that the vehicles are in good working order and that adequate insurance (with collision damage waiver) is provided before making a commitment.
- Use an **international car rental company** if you intend to travel long distances as more comprehensive support will be offered if you break down. One-way rentals are available only with multinational companies.
- You can **book your car before you travel** and have it waiting for you when you arrive at the airport.
- You'll receive a quote in pounds sterling or US dollars and pay in Turkish lira. **Credit cards are required** at the time of hire in lieu of a cash deposit.
- **Fuel** is sold by the litre in unleaded and leaded form. Filling stations are not usually self-service, and your windscreen may be cleaned for you at no extra charge. Some petrol stations do not accept credit cards.

Driving

- You won't need to drive in Istanbul but **a car is useful for touring** the Turkish coast.
- **Drive on the right** and overtake on the left.
- **Speed limits** are 50kph (30mph) in urban areas, 90kph (55mph) on other highways and 120kph (75mph) on motorways and expressways.
- **Seat belts** are compulsory in front seats, and in back seats where fitted.
- **Road surfaces** are generally acceptable and road signs conform to international agreements.
- City streets are busy but country roads tend to be quiet. On **country roads**, be aware of slow-moving farm vehicles and animals.
- **Traffic lights** may intermittently flash orange when traffic is light, indicating that vehicles can proceed in either direction if nothing is coming.
- Do not park where there are yellow-painted kerbstones.

- **Maps** covering the major roads and sites can be picked up at car rental offices.
- Many Turks pull off the road to the right before turning left rather than holding traffic up behind them. It is common practice to **drive on the hard shoulder** to let faster traffic pass – but beware of potholes and debris.
- The **Turkish Touring and Automobile Association** (TTOK or Turing; Oto, Sanayi Sitesi Yanı, 4 Levent, Istanbul, tel: 0212 282 8140; www.turing.org.tr) provides rescue services.

Admission Prices
The cost of admission for places of interest is indicated by price categories:
Inexpensive under 3YTL
Moderate 3–6YTL
Expensive more than 6YTL

Accommodation

Accommodation Prices
The once volatile Turkish Lira has been replaced with the more stable New Turkish Lira, but Turks still have the habit of pricing accommodation in another currency, usually the Euro or US Dollar, so there's no need to change your cash in advance at a bureaux de change as your hotel will be happy to accept it in payment for accommodation, although any change will be paid to you in local currency.

Booking Accommodation
Accommodation in this guide is rated £, ££ and £££, which denotes the price band within which you should expect to pay per night for a double or twin room with a private bathroom.

- Establishments recommended in the **£ category** (up to $130) are usually *pansiyons* (pensions), most of which are family-run. *Pansiyons* vary greatly in terms of standards and facilities offered, but will always have at least some sort of room or terrace where breakfast is taken. Many *pansiyons* can also be persuaded to offer an evening meal, which can be a wonderful opportunity to taste bargain-priced Turkish home-cooking. Usually, the more remote the *pansiyon*, the greater the chance you have of being cooked dinner. If dinner is not available, your hosts will be happy to recommend somewhere modest and local, where you should mention your *pansiyon*'s name by way of introduction (and to ensure a fair bill).
- The majority of places recommended in this guide fall into the **££ category** ($130–$230). Many of the **hotels** in this category offer extraordinary value for money, and you may well find yourself enjoying all manner of facilities, from swimming-pools to Turkish Baths (known as *hamam*). This price band also covers many of the newly fashionable "resort-hotels" which pride themselves on being self-sufficient. While such places can be wonderful for families with children, you may find that you feel a little isolated from real Turkish culture. You may also pay above the odds for extras, particularly drinks. It's always a good idea to

agree in advance how much drinks and other extras will cost, especially if you intend to charge them to your room. This will avoid any nasty surprises at check-out time. If you have been signing for extras, never accept a global figure when you check-out, but ask to see copies of all the chits that you've signed, just as any Turk would. It's all too easy for mistakes to be made and you could find that you are paying for someone else's extras as well as your own. Don't be embarrassed to ask!

- Most hotels in the **£££ category** (over $230 per night) will consider themselves to be ritzy indeed and will expect you to maintain their standards too! Dress codes will usually apply, as will service charges and just about every service will be a chargeable "extra". Staff will expect tips commensurate with your being rich enough to afford a place that costs more for a night than many of them earn in a fortnight, but don't let this put you off: at Turkish prices, you will still be enjoying 5-star luxury at a fraction of what you could expect to pay at home.

Bargaining

Accommodation prices in Turkey are somewhat flexible, with differences between high- and low-seaon rates, and often between rates for Turks and rates for foreign visitors. Bargaining is a way of life in Turkey and is conducted according to time-honoured bargaining rules outlined below.

- Never accept the first price that you are quoted. Smile sweetly and explain that the price is too high, and please can you have a better one.
- Offer between 50 per cent and 70 per cent of that price and then stick to your guns for a while. Your aim should be to achieve what you believe to be a fair price, that neither embarrasses the hotel-keeper nor you. Understand, however, that a well-run, busy establishment with a good reputation has less need to quote highly inflated prices in the first place or to reduce them subsequently.
- Always keep your sense of humour about you, even though others may feign anger – you'll be the best of friends once the deal is concluded. Also, you'll get the best out of a deal if the receptionist or manager that you're dealing with is not run off his or her feet, and has time to negotiate with you. It may pay you to offer to sit somewhere and wait for your host to be ready for you, than to try and steamroller a deal.
- When you're near to reaching an agreement, remember that a clincher will always be your ability to pay in foreign currency cash. If you intend to pay by credit card, be aware that some places (usually out of the main resorts) may attempt add a surcharge of up to 3 per cent.
- Always agree in advance exactly what the negotiated price includes. Some (deluxe) hotels have a habit of adding 18 per cent "tax" onto bills. Others may sting you extra for breakfast.
- Most resort hotels will insist on dinner being taken in the hotel's restaurant in season. Often this adds only about $10 to the cost of the room, so you won't have to feel too guilty about skipping the buffet in order to try other restaurants.
- Room prices are affected by the length of time you intend to stay, and the time of year that you visit. In essence, the longer your stay, the lower the daily rate you should expect to pay. It can be a useful bargaining position to agree a daily rate, then to negotiate a lower price for a longer stay.
- Once you have agreed the price, the method of payment, the duration of stay and what the rate includes, ask to see the room. You may find that you've been negotiating for a windowless mosquito-breeding station or possibly for a suite fit for a sultan. Never feel pressured to accept a room that you don't like – remember that Turks will refuse at least two rooms before settling on their choice. The keywords here are calm and courtesy.

Food and Drink

Eating is one of the chief pleasures of visiting Turkey, and Turks take their wonderful food almost for granted. A combination of kind climates and fertile soils enable the country to be more or less self-sufficient – this makes ingredients (and consequently eating out) relatively inexpensive. Food is the concrete that binds Turkish society, and you'll see local people enthusiastically buying and eating food everywhere, on the streets, at cafés and at restaurants in former palaces.

Specialities

- **Breakfast** can go on for hours, and typically includes oceans of (black) tea (tea with milk is *sütli çay*, pronounced "sootlu chayi"), warm bread, white cheese, olives, tomato, cucumber, a hard-boiled egg, jam and honey.
- **Snacking** is an art-form – from brown-paper bags of excellent *fistik* (pistachios), *cekiderk* (pumpkin seeds) and luscious dried fruits from Kuruyemis shops, to street-vendor-sold *simit* (large, soft, bagel-shaped breads, covered in sesame seeds), to rich and chewy *dondurma* (ice-cream), sometimes sold in freshly made, warm cones.
- *Mezze* are cold or hot starters that are offered in most restaurants. You can make a selection of both for *hors d'oeuvres* but go easy on the excellent *pide* (bread) that accompanies them, or you'll have no room for anything else. *Mezze* also make meals in themselves and are an excellent option for vegetarians. You'll either choose your *mezze*, chaperoned by a waiter, from a glassed-in fridge, or have them brought to your table on trays. Ask questions before you point, or it will be assumed that you have made your choice and the plates will be put in front of you immediately.
- **Soup** (*çorbasɪ*) is a national passion, with *mercimek* (lentil) and *yayla* (yoghurt and rice) soups particularly popular. İşkembeci restaurants specialise in *İşkembe* (tripe) and *paça* (sheep tongue and foot) soups and are usually open all night, their stomach-wrenching creations being thought to cure hangovers.
- **Fish** is relatively expensive. If you're offered a whole fish between everyone at the table, always agree a price with the waiter first. If you're quoted a price per kilo, ask to see the fish being weighed.
- Turkish food relies on the freshness of its ingredients, so fish and meat are best **served plain**, either fried, grilled or roasted.
- Turkey is the spiritual home of the grilled meat **kebab**. You can often choose from a display of different meats; otherwise, the waiter will tell you what's available. *Döner* is the lamb (or chicken) cylinder whirring in the window. It may also be offered as *işkender*, served on a base of cut bread and covered in tomato and yoghurt. *Köfte* are patties of grilled lamb – *Adana köfte* are spicy versions. *Şiş* are lamb cubes, while *cöpşış* are smaller, often even more tender, pieces.
- **Salads** should be ordered in addition to the main dish, although *ocakbaşis* (▶ Dining Options, 34) usually serve mounds of salad with their grills. Ask for *çoban* (mixed) salad, and tell the waiter whether you prefer it without onions (*soğansɪz*, pronounced "soansuz"). Beware: the long, thin green peppers featured in most salads might be very mild – or they might be very hot!
- **Fruit and vegetables** are amazingly fresh and bursting with flavour. Turkish tomatoes, for example, no matter how knobbled and knarled, are especially sweet, and the delicious taste of fruits such as cherries, apricots and peaches lingers on your tongue long after you've finished eating.

■ **Desserts** are not a strength of most restaurants, although pastry shops and *muhallebici* (specialising in milk-based desserts) abound. Instead, *karpuz* (watermelon) or other fruits are offered, together with thimblefuls of murky *kahve* (**coffee**). When ordering, state whether you prefer it *sade* (without sugar), *orta* (medium) or *şekerli* (very sugary). You'll notice that the bottom third of the cup is muddy coffee grounds, which you won't want to drink.

Drink Specialities

■ Although the majority of Turks are Muslims, Turkey is a secular state (➤ 9–11) and moderate alcoholic consumption is permitted. Local **Efes beer** is good, and **wines** from Villa Doluca and Kavaklıdere are reliable.

■ **Soft drinks** come in all forms, or try refreshing, yoghurt-based *ayran* with a kebab. Fresh juices are often offered, both in bars and from street-side *bufe* (buffet) – treat yourself to an intensely fruity *portakal* (orange) or a darkly sweet *vişne* (black cherry) juice.

■ **Rakı**, based on raisins and aniseed and known as "lion's milk", is the national spirit. Be wary of its potency and take your lead from the locals, sipping it slowly, diluting it further as you go, and interspersing sips with plenty of *mezze*.

Dining Options

■ *Restoran*: restaurant, usually with linen, wine lists and professional service. *Lokanta*: Usually slightly more informal and less expensive than a *restoran*.

■ *Kebab salonu*: These (sometimes strip-lit, often unsentimental) places are frequented by workers and families alike, and are usually to be relied on for cheap and tasty meals. Many offer a hot table of stews and casseroles, with which you'll be offered *pilav* (rice) or sometimes *burghul* (cracked wheat).

■ *Ocakbasi*: Kurdish-inspired open grills, around which you can sit (tables are also available) plus an array of *mezze* – great for relaxed dining.

■ *Meyhane*: Mostly in cities, these taverns tend to be evening-only, and usually offer live music.

■ *Pide salonu*: Turkish pizza houses – try *lahmacun* for vanishingly thin dough and meat or vegetable toppings, while *pide* has a more bready texture, and often feature cheese and butter toppings, sometimes with the addition of *sujuk* (dried beef sausage).

A Practical Guide to Eating Out

■ You can dine really well for $20 or less per person, including soft drinks and service. Wine can easily add another $5 per head.

■ Eating hours are: **breakfast** from about 7 to 11, **lunch** from 11:30 to 4, and **dinner** from 5:30 to midnight. Most cafés, *bufes*, *lokantas* and restaurants are open continuously throughout the day, every day, and will only close when the last person leaves.

■ In busy tourist areas, or for waterfront tables, **call ahead to reserve**. In other establishments, space will nearly always be found for you on arrival.

■ Even though service is often included, **a tip of 10 per cent** will elicit big smiles and make you especially popular.

■ The majority of places recommended in this guide are happy to accept credit cards (though not always American Express and Diners), although some might charge up to 5 per cent commission for the service. If paying in cash, American dollars are never unwelcome.

■ Many Turks **smoke** and a request for a non-smoking table will usually be met with polite disbelief.

Shopping

Keen shoppers will be delighted with the variety of goods available across the country. Turkey has a legacy of exceptional skill in handicrafts and supplements these traditions by keeping an eye on the latest Western trends.

The Turkish Bazaar

The bazaar is the traditional marketplace of Turkey and Istanbul's Kapalıçarşı (Grand Bazaar, ► 49–50 and 59) is the greatest of them all.

Most larger towns and resorts have similar markets on a smaller scale. The best are at **İzmir** (► 78), noted for its high-quality handicrafts; **Fethiye** (► 128), which is small and stylish, with high-quality leather goods and jewellery; **Kaş** (► 128), the place to go for bohemian jewellery and great carpets. Also worth seeking out are the bazaars at **Kuşadası** (► 105), which caters for tourists, with a predominance of fake designer labels; **Side** (► 154) for souvenirs, from handicrafts to designer gear, and **Alanya** (► 154), perfect for stocking up on cheap T-shirts and socks.

Traditional Goods
Hand-knotted **carpets** in wool, silk and cotton, and handwoven *kilims* (flat-weave rugs)
Leather goods, especially jackets, trousers, shoes and bags
Hand-crafted gold and silver **jewellery** (including designer watches)
Onyx and alabaster carved into bowls, candlesticks, vases, goblets and ornaments
Meerschaum – a soft rock that's normally carved into pipes
Coffee tables and backgammon boards made from **carved and inlaid wood**
Brass and copper cooking vessels and crockery
Textiles, especially richly decorated blankets and cushions
Edibles such as *lokum* (Turkish delight), spices, honey and apple tea

---

Haggling

Shopping in bazaars can be an enjoyable experience – in carpet shops, for example, you'll be invited to sit and take apple tea while you buy. Remember though, that **browsing is not encouraged**, and the hard sell can get a little wearing, so keep your sense of humour and don't be intimidated.

Few prices in Turkish bazaars are fixed, so you'll need to **bargain**. Never accept the initial asking price. You should end up paying around **50 to 70 per cent** of the first price suggested, depending on your skill and patience, but bear in mind that some vendors start with ridiculous mark-ups, while others stay close to their final price. **Never mention a price you are not prepared to pay**, as the seller will no doubt stick to that.

Paying

- **Credit cards** are not universally accepted, though the larger stores will accept them.
- Some shops will add an **extra fee** if you pay by credit card.
- **Inflation has been a major problem in recent times** in Turkey so you may get a better deal if you pay in US dollars, Sterling or Euros.
- **Large or expensive purchases** will always be charged in a foreign currency, usually US dollars.
- **Traveller's cheques** are not accepted in shops.

Entertainment

Turkey's varied entertainment programme is centred on the major resorts, and tourists are welcomed to many of the cultural and sporting events that are held throughout the year.

Finding Out What's On

There are no regular "what's on" magazines covering the Turkish coast, and tourist offices in resorts have a mixed reputation for helpfulness. To find out the exact dates and ticketing details for events described below, contact the Turkish Government Tourist Office in your own country (➤ 170–171).

Festivals and Events

- The arts calendar is full during the summer. The most accessible event to visitors is the **Aspendos Opera and Ballet Festival** (➤ 154), held in June and featuring the stars of the opera world.
- There are also a number of **folkloric and music festivals** featuring groups from all around the country. The best is the **İzmir International Festival** (➤ 106), mid-June to mid-July.
- Istanbul has a series of festivals running between April and November, including the **International Istanbul Music Festival** in June and July and the **Istanbul Jazz Festival** in July.

Sporting Events

- Traditional Turkish sports such as grease wrestling (➤ 22–23) and camel wrestling (➤ panel, page 23) are becoming more difficult to find, but a busy programme of **competitive sports** takes place along the coast. The main **camel wrestling** competition is in January (when the camels are in rut) in Selçuk (➤ 88–89), and if you want to see grease wrestling make your way to Elmalı (➤ 128) during the first week in September.
- If **sailing competitions** are more your thing, you can watch the sails unfurl at the International Yachting Festival in Marmaris in May, the International Bodrum Cup (➤ 106) in October and international yacht racing in November, again in Marmaris.
- The **Formula 1 Grand Prix** is held at the circuit just outside Istanbul in May each year.

Outdoor Activities

- Turkey offers **a wealth of outdoor activities**, including cycling, walking, mountaineering, horseback-riding, sailing, spelunking (exploring caves), diving, skiing, rafting, kayaking and canoeing, off-road safaris and tandem parasailing. A range of water sports are available at the main resorts, such as windsurfing, waterskiing and banana-boat rides.
- **Boat rides**, available from all harbours along the Turkish coast, are a must. Don't forget to take a swimsuit for swimming and snorkelling. You can also take **day trips** to several Greek islands in the Aegean; Rhodes (➤ panel, page 120) is particularly interesting but any Greek island offers a fascinating contrast to Turkish culture.

Nightlife

- Nightlife, based around music bars and clubs, can be **loud and lively** in major resorts.
- In smaller resorts and in the countryside, evening entertainment is **more subdued** and centres on an evening meal and a few drinks.

Istanbul and the Western Black Sea Coast

Getting Your Bearings

Mysterious and romantic, Istanbul's domes and minarets are famed all over the world. This is literally where East meets West: the city sits astride the Bosphorus Strait, the continental divide between Europe and Asia. It's both an amazing historical treasure trove and Turkey's most vibrant and modern city, the intellectual and business hub of the republic.

At Your Leisure

Most of the major historical monuments are found in the tiny old capital district – Sultanahmet – where the city of Byzantium became Christian Constantinople and then Islamic Istanbul. A magnet for tourists and easy to explore, its attractions are close together among sculpted parks and squares. A 15-minute stroll west leads to the Grand Bazaar, which is surrounded by a maze of narrow, crowded shopping streets, and beyond is Süleymaniye Mosque, the epitome of Islamic architecture.

To feel the pulse of modern Istanbul, do as the locals do and take the five-minute ferry ride from Eminönü waterfront, north across the Golden Horn waterway to the old diplomatic neighbourhood, now the heart of the modern city around adjoining Beyoğlu and Taksim districts. Here, you can ride the funicular from the north shore to medieval Galata Tower for panoramic cityscapes, before plunging back into the bustle of city life amid the boutiques, eateries, bars and nightclubs.

Two city attractions are best reached by taxi – florid Dolmabahçe Palace along the waterfront to the northeast, and the superlative mosaics of the Byzantine Kariye Camii, to the west.

10 Kariye Camii

FENE

FEVZİ PAŞA CADDESİ

★ **Don't Miss**

1. **Aya Sofya Camii (Haghia Sophia Basilica)** ➤ 42
2. **Sultanahmet Camii (Blue Mosque)** ➤ 44
3. **Topkapı Sarayı (Topkapı Palace)** ➤ 46
4. **Kapalıçarşı (Grand Bazaar)** ➤ 49

Roman exhibit in the Arkeoloji Müzesi

Further Afield

15. Şile ➤ 56
16. Safranbolu ➤ 56

Page 37: Aya Sofya Camii

A boat tour on the Bosphorus is a welcome contrast to dusty streets, or leave the city for the Black Sea resort of Şile. If you have more time to spare, the Ottoman town of Safranbolu, 400km (250 miles) from Istanbul is worth the journey. Little changed in 250 years, it boasts some wonderful architecture.

Below: 17th-century Sultanahmet Camii still dominates the city's skyline

Istanbul combines East and West, ancient and modern, action and relaxation. Spend the days exploring the architectural and cultural gems of the city and the nights enjoying the Turkish traditions of the *hamam* and belly dancing.

Istanbul in Two Days

Day 1

Morning

Get up as early as possible to make the most of the morning light filtering through the upper windows of **1 Aya Sofya Camii** (➤ 42–43). Take your time admiring the magnificent 6th-century basilica, its columns, galleries and mosaics. Then take a short stroll across the formal gardens to the early-17th century **2 Sultanahmet Camii** (➤ 44–45; also known as the Blue Mosque), to marvel at its sleek tile decoration. Eat lunch on street of the old city, or at the ancient race circuit of the lies just beyond the walls of

architectural lines and intricate Divan Yolu Caddesi, the arterial Hipodrom (Hippodrome), the Byzantine emperors, which Sultanahmet Camii.

Afternoon

Take an intimate look at the daily life of the Ottoman sultans by touring the vast **8 Topkapı Sarayı** (Topkapı Palace, ➤ 46–48), which was their home for more than 300 years. You'll need the whole afternoon to admire the marvellous array of jewels collected from the Ottoman Empire, to visit the Divan Pavilion where major political decisions were made, and to discover how the wives and concubines of the sultan spent their time in the harem.

Evening

If you're feeling jaded after a long day sightseeing, take a Turkish bath at the Çemberlitaş Hamami (➤ 157), which is just behind Çemberlitaş (➤ 157). Built in marble by the same architect who designed Süleymaniye Camii, it has separate sections for men and women and is open from 6am until midnight every day.

Day 2

Morning

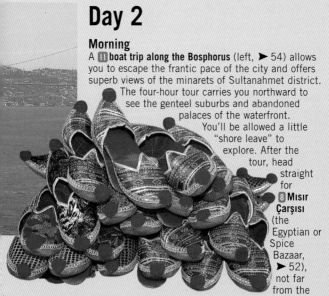

A **11 boat trip along the Bosphorus** (left, ➤ 54) allows you to escape the frantic pace of the city and offers superb views of the minarets of Sultanahmet district. The four-hour tour carries you northward to see the genteel suburbs and abandoned palaces of the waterfront. You'll be allowed a little "shore leave" to explore. After the tour, head straight for **9 Mısır Çarşısı** (the Egyptian or Spice Bazaar, ➤ 52), not far from the boat dock, to Pandelli restaurant, on its upper floor, one of the finest eateries in the city.

Afternoon

Make your way through to the labyrinthine streets of **4 Kapalıçarşı** (the Grand Bazaar, ➤ 49–50), where goods of every description, from jewellery. leatherware and crafts (above), await. Have your shopping list and money at the ready.

Evening

Make your way across the Golden Horn to the top of the **12 Galata Kulesi** (Galata Tower, ➤ 54) and have your camera ready as you watch the sun set behind the minarets of Sultanahmet. After nightfall visit a belly dancing show, or dinner and folkloric performances at Orient House (➤ 60).

❶ Aya Sofya Camii
(Haghia Sophia Basilica)

Decorated with dazzling Byzantine mosaics, Aya Sofya Camii uniquely combines breathtaking Christian and Islamic architecture. It's also rich in historical significance: on its inauguration in the 6th century, the "Church of the Divine Wisdom" was regarded as the seat of God's power on earth. Converted into a mosque when Constantinople fell to Islamic forces, its graceful lines became a blueprint for religious buildings throughout the Ottoman Empire.

When Aya Sofya was constructed in AD532, Emperor Justinian ordered that no expense be spared. The church was to be the glittering jewel in Christianity's crown, a symbol of the Byzantine Empire's wealth and power. Justinian trawled the ancient sites of Asia Minor in search of materials, looting

The domes and minarets of Aya Sofya Camii rise majestically skywards

several columns from the Temple of Artemis in Ephesus (► panel, page 85), and employed the best mosaic and fresco artists to decorate the interior. His creation, with a huge unsupported central dome and open colonnades, was unequalled for more than a millennium. When Islamic forces arrived in 1453, the church was saved from demolition but, though its basic design remained intact, four minarets were built on its outer corners. The interior icons, unacceptable to Muslim beliefs, were plastered over, inadvertently preserving them until restoration in the late 19th century exposed their splendour. Aya Sofya became a museum in the 1930s.

Attention to Detail

The modern entrance into Aya Sofya is from the **west door of the narthex** (entrance hall). The narthex is covered with magnificent mosaics, dating from the 6th to the 11th centuries, and gilded panels decorated with floral designs and geometric patterns. At the centre of the narthex is the ornate **Imperial Gate**, the ceremonial entryway during Byzantine

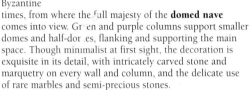

The Weeping Column

In the northwest corner of the aisle stands the "Weeping Column". According to Christian legend, Emperor Justinian cured his headache by resting his forehead against the moist, cool marble. The hole that was subsequently worn through by thousands of pilgrims certainly helped Mehmet II when he took the city in 1453. A Muslim legend relates how he put his finger in the hole and turned the church towards Mecca so that it could be converted into a mosque.

times, from where the full majesty of the **domed nave** comes into view. Green and purple columns support smaller domes and half-domes, flanking and supporting the main space. Though minimalist at first sight, the decoration is exquisite in its detail, with intricately carved stone and marquetry on every wall and column, and the delicate use of rare marbles and semi-precious stones.

Artistic Treasures

A ramp leads from the nave to the tribunes (upper galleries) and it is here that **the main wealth of mosaics** has been revealed. Dating from between the 10th and the 14th centuries, this collection is among the most artistically accomplished and historically important in the world. The **southern tribune** – once reserved for the Byzantine royal family – has the richest decoration and shows dynasties of emperors and empresses consulting Christ and the Virgin Mary. In historical terms, the mosaics are a "who's who" of Byzantine royalty, showing the line of descent over many generations. The skilful craftsmanship, too, is notable, with clever use of gold and gemstones and the use of smaller tesserae to show fine shading and perspective in the later mosaics. The **Deësis ("Prayer") mosaics**, beyond a marble doorway at the end of the gallery, are particularly detailed, with the faces of Jesus, Mary and John the Baptist expressing a serene dignity.

The Deësis mosaics are much admired for their fine craftsmanship

🚇 179 C2 ✉ Aya Sofya Meydanı, Sultanahmet 🕐 Tue–Sun 9:20–4:30
🚊 Sultanahmet 💲 Expensive

AYA SOFYA CAMII: INSIDE INFO

Top tip To be able to see the fine detail of the high domes and columns you'll need to **take binoculars**.

In more depth Before entering the precinct, walk through **the courtyard garden** where you'll see the old kitchens and ablutions fountain to the left and tombs of Ottoman sultans to the right.

② Sultanahmet Camii
(Blue Mosque)

Begun in 1609 on the site of the old Byzantine palace, Sultanahmet Camii was intended to rival the great Aya Sofya Camii (► 42–43) and Süleymaniye Camii (► 53), and still dominates the skyline of the Sultanahmet district today. Around 20,000 azure İznik tiles decorate its interior, quickly leading worshippers to nickname it the Blue Mosque.

The formal entry into the mosque complex is from the Hippodrome to the west (► 156–158), through the main entrance into the courtyard. However, most visitors approach from Aya Sofya, walking across Aya Sofya Meydanı, the square to the northeast of the mosque. From here, you can best take in the panorama of Sultanahmet Camii's pale, marble walls and myriad domes, looming over the ornamental garden. Once in the **courtyard** with its ornate ritual ablutions fountain, make your way around to the entrance set aside for non-Muslims, on the northern flank of the mosque.

The scale of the mosque is most striking in the **prayer room.** Its marble interior and 260 windows reflect light into the central prayer area, giving the illusion of even greater height to its 43m (140-foot) **dome.** The dome is supported by four pillars 5m (16 feet) in diameter, known as the "elephant paws" because of their enormous size and splayed bases. Thousands of beautiful **blue tiles**, delicately painted with floral and abstract designs, line the walls, and these are enhanced by blue stencil decoration on the curved surfaces of the domes and arches. The oldest and most magnificent tiles are set under the arches of the arcades surrounding the prayer area but because these recesses are unlit the tiles cannot be seen to best effect.

A carved marble **mihrab** (niche indicating the direction of Mecca) and *minbar* (pulpit) of fine Marmara marble can be seen on the far wall beyond the barrier that separates the public from the *haram* or prayer area.

TAKING A BREAK

Outside the mosque complex on the western flank of Sultanahmet you'll find inexpensive **traditional cafés** selling Turkish tea and coffee, where you can relax on low settees and watch the world go by.

The towering cupolas of Sultanahmet Camii are supported by massive columns with huge splayed bases

The Legacy of İznik Tiles

The mosque was built at a time when tile production in the town of İznik, to the southwest of Istanbul, was at its peak. From the 15th century, İznik was the centre of all things ceramic, its potteries turning out endless wall tiles for Ottoman building projects in Istanbul. The distinctive style was created by painting plants, flowers, fruit, geometric patterns and fashionable Chinese motifs in vivid blues on dazzling white tiles. Later, turquoise, purple, green and red were added to the palette. By the late 17th century, however, İznik's glory had faded, but recent efforts by various Turkish organisations are helping to revive some of the old designs.

🔢 179 C2
✉ Atmeydanı Sok (Hipodrom), Sultanahmet
🕐 Daily dawn to dusk except prayer times (▶ Top tips, below);
Royal Pavilion: Tue–Sun 9–noon
🚇 Sultanahmet
💷 Free; Royal Pavilion: inexpensive

SULTANAHMET CAMII: INSIDE INFO

Top tips All mosques are **closed to non-Muslims between 1pm and about 3pm on Fridays,** during the main prayer time of the week. Shorter, daily prayer times, announced by the call of the *muezzin,* usually last about 15 minutes. If you are not a Muslim, just wait outside the mosque until prayers have finished.
• Between May and September a free nightly sound-and-light show takes place in the ornamental gardens between the mosque and Aya Sofya.

In more depth There is an fine collection of knotted carpets, some dating back to the 16th century, in the **Royal Pavilion** in the complex's northeastern corner.

3 Topkapı Sarayı
(Topkapı Palace)

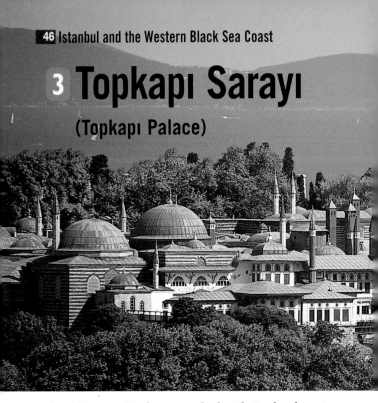

For 400 years, Topkapı was the legislative headquarters, diplomatic centre and family palace of the powerful Ottoman sultans. This outstanding example of Ottoman secular architecture is now an important museum housing exceptional collections of jewellery, porcelain and armoury.

Begun in the late 15th century, the enormous palace is located in a commanding position overlooking the waterways of the city. It was divided into a number of separate "courts" or areas, each with a specific function. Today, the first court is public parkland and the main entrance to the palace is at the gateway to the second courtyard.

The Second Courtyard

Once through the tight security procedures, you'll find yourself in the large Second Courtyard, with its formal gardens. You'll see the former stables (on the left) and the enormous kitchens, now used to display one of the finest collections of Chinese porcelain and silverware in the world (on the right). Also in this courtyard is the **Divan Pavilion**. Highly decorated with a mosaic of blue tiles, this small chamber was where important political decisions were

✚ 179 D3
✉ Sultanahmet. Walk by the right flank of Aya Sofya and through the gate of the first courtyard
☎ www.topkapisarayi.gov.tr ⏰ May–Sep Wed–Mon 9–7; Oct–Apr 9–5 🚊 Sultanahmet
💷 Expensive
Harem guided tours
⏰ Wed–Mon 9:30–3:30; depart every 20 minutes 💷 Expensive

made by the imperial council.
The grand vizier (chief advisor) chaired meetings from a
couch or divan (hence the
pavilion's name), while the
sultan kept an eye on
proceedings from behind a
grille still seen in the wall.

The Second Courtyard also
leads to the entrance to the
harem of the sultans. The
word "harem" refers to
private rooms in any Muslim
house, but here it was the
part of the palace reserved
exclusively for the sultan's
wives, concubines, children
and servants. The harem at
Topkapı is made up of 300
rooms; a veritable palace
within a palace. The guided
tour of the harem covers only
a small part of its total area
but is nonetheless an essential part of your visit. The
ornate decoration throughout, particularly within the
**Sultan's Salon, Salon
of Murat III** (with its
beautiful İznik tiles)
and **Ahmet III's room**
(decorated with exquisite
paintings of fruit and flowers), is
undoubtedly the finest in the
palace, a testament to the skill of
artisans of the time. The tour guides
will bring it all to life with their stories
of the characters who used to
live there.

The Third Courtyard

After your tour of the
harem, you'll exit into
the Third Courtyard.
Here, you'll find the
most precious objects
of the Ottoman
Empire. On the
right-hand flank is
the **Treasury**,
which displays a
spectacular
collection of
precious stones
and metals. Among
the riches here are

The vast
palace
complex
(above)
houses many
treasures,
including
displays of
armour

The splendid interior of the Hünkar Sofası (Hall of the Emperor) in the harem

three solid gold thrones, the 86-carat Spoonmaker's Diamond and the emerald-encrusted Topkapı Dagger (the thieves' objective in the 1964 film *Topkapi*).

On the left-hand side of the Third Courtyard (looking from the gate) is the **Pavilion of the Holy Mantle**. This displays the sacred relics accumulated by Selim the Grim when he conquered Egypt in 1517. These include a footprint of the prophet Mohammed, left in the sand as he ascended to heaven, and a box containing hairs from his beard.

Life in the Harem

When a woman entered the harem she was not allowed to leave its confines until at least nine years had passed. Many were foreign slaves who had been taken as young girls and trained to be concubines (sexual companions) to the sultan. Contrary to modern myth, concubines were not necessarily degraded by their status – it was at least a more luxurious life than that in the outside world. Women received particular favours if the sultan took a liking to them or if they bore him a son. In the latter stages of Ottoman rule, the unprecedented elevation of Roxelana to become wife of Süleyman the Magnificent (▶ 17) enabled some women to exert a political influence, and the harem became something of a power base within the palace.

TAKING A BREAK

The **Fourth Courtyard** comprises a series of gardens puncuated with grassy lawns, rosebeds and a number of *köskü* (pavilions). This was a private area where the sultan could relax. The elegant Mecidiye Köşkü or Abdülmahcid Köşkü now houses **Konyalı**, an excellent, if pricey, restaurant where you can take lunch while enjoying the excellent views over the city and along the Bosphorus.

TOPKAPI SARAYI: INSIDE INFO

Top tips There is only space for 60 people on the 30-minute **harem tour**, so book your place as soon as you arrive. After entering the second courtyard, make your way to the left, across the gardens, to buy your ticket. You will be given a time to return for your tour.

• It takes around **three hours** to see the palace's highlights (including the harem, Divan Pavilion and Treasury) but allow a full day if you want to take in the entire complex.

In more depth Take time to enjoy the **excellent collections** of porcelain, armaments, manuscripts, tapestries and costumes in different parts of the palace – each could easily be a stand-alone museum.

▣ Kapalıçarşı
(Grand Bazaar)

The original – and still the ultimate – shopping mall, this vaulted labyrinth of 3,500 shops has been purveying the best Eastern merchandise for more than 650 years. Crammed with goods, it's a fascinating place to explore whether you're looking to spend a little, a lot, or nothing at all.

The bazaar built its reputation during the early years of the Ottoman era when the expanding empire traded goods from India, China and Africa. Great quantities of gold, silver and precious stones were stored in the *bedesten*, the covered and lockable area that forms the bazaar's central core. In those days, the bazaar was not just a market but also a vast workshop, with each trade founding its own *han* (quarter or courtyard) as a centre of expertise for hundreds of skilled artisans. Today, most of the workshops have moved out, leaving the bazaar to the sales people – and a very persuasive group they are too. You'll need to accept that Turkish sales tactics are very different from the European and American

The covered streets of Kapalıçarşı offer a treasure trove of souvenirs

ethos of self-service so don't feel intimidated by their attention, or by the rush of people filling the bazaar's narrow alleyways.

Orientation

There are more than 20 entrances to the Grand Bazaar but the most popular and easy to find is the **Nuruosmaniye Kapisi** or Gate, next to the Nuruosmaniye Mosque. Once through the gate you'll find yourself on **Kalpakçılar Başi Caddesi**, the longest street in the bazaar, which is renowned for its leather goods. A little way along this road, on the right, is **Kuyumcular Caddesi**, the main jewellery area, where you'll see shimmering displays of gold. Here you can find original Turkish designs and copies of Italian and French fashions. If you walk to the top of Kalpakçılar Başi Caddesi, you'll find ceramics on **Yağlıkçılar Caddesi** to the right. The best carpet shops are on three parallel streets to the north of Kalpakçılar Başi Caddesi – **Halıcılar Çarşısı Caddesi**, **Takkeciler Sok** and **Keseciler Caddesi** – though you'll find lower-quality carpets in practically every alley.

> ### Haggle away!
> Haggling (➤ 35) is a way of life in Turkey and few items have fixed prices so you'll need to hone your bargaining skills. Haggling is just a process of negotiation and should be fun, not daunting. At the end of the day, as long as you're happy with the price you paid, it doesn't matter whether someone else has bought the same item for a little less.

TAKING A BREAK

If it's lunch you're after, try **Padaliza** on Yağlıkçılar Caddesi, which offers excellent Turkish cuisine in a refurbished *han*. For a shorter break, head to the traditional **Şark Kahvesi**, also on Yağlıkçılar Caddesi, where you can drink coffee and tea, play backgammon and try a *hookah* pipe.

✚ 179 C2 ✉ Off Yeniçeriler Caddesi 🕐 May–Oct daily 9–7; Nov–Apr 9–6 🚇 Çemberlitaş
🎫 Free

KAPALIÇARŞI: INSIDE INFO

Top tips Foreign currency in cash will always have more bargaining power than credit cards, but there are **ATM machines** within the bazaar if you run out of Turkish lira.

• **Don't worry about following a set route** around the bazaar or getting lost. You'll enjoy your visit more if you wander wherever your interests and shopping desires take you.

• **Shopping early or late in the day may get you a better deal.** An early first sale indicates a fortuitous day ahead for the salesman so he may be more flexible on cost. A late sale is an unexpected bonus for him so you may be able to wrangle a lower price by walking away – few shopkeepers will turn cash down if you are their last customer.

At Your Leisure

A detail of a sarcophagi frieze in the Arkeoloji Müzesi

5 Arkeoloji Müzesi (Archaeological Museum)

Tucked away in the first courtyard of Topkapı Palace (▶ 46–48), and almost unnoticed among the palace's wealth of riches, the Archaeological Museum could occupy you for an entire afternoon, but the highlights can be viewed in around an hour.

It's a large complex comprising three buildings and a courtyard garden. The excellent **Museum of the Ancient Orient**, next to the ticket office, displays an impressive collection of objects relating to the development of the Anatolian, Mesopotamian and Hittite civilisations of Turkey, along with artefacts from Egypt. Pride of place in this modern gallery is given to the Treaty of Kadesh, the world's oldest extant peace treaty. Across the courtyard, the **original museum** building houses a set of exquisite carved sarcophagi found in Sidon in 1887.

These are displayed to great effect in subdued light in the northern wing of the ground floor. The southern wing displays statuary found at Greek and Roman sites around Asia Minor.

The diminutive **Çinili Köşk,** dating from 1472, displays a small selection of fine ceramics, including several priceless pieces from İznik.

🚹 179 D2 ✉ First Courtyard, Topkapı Palace 🕓 Tue–Sun 9:30–5 🚇 Sultanahmet 💵 Moderate

6 Türk ve İslam Eserleri Müzesi (Museum of Turkish and Islamic Art)

This collection brings together some of the finest examples of different Eastern arts. From ceramics to brassware, carved stone to glassware, manuscripts to carpets and textiles, the museum displays more than 40,000 items dating from the 7th to the early 20th century.

Housed on the first floor of the renovated Palace of İbrahim Paşa – a gift from Süleyman the Magnificent to his grand vizier (principal advisor) in 1520 – the pieces are effectively displayed, particularly in the large carpet halls, and accompanied by informative text in English. Downstairs, there's a small but well-organised ethnographic collection where you can see re-creations of various traditional Turkish dwellings, including

a nomad's *yurt* (tent), a stone hut and a 19th-century Ottoman town house.

🕇 179 C2 ✉ İbrahim Paşa Sarayı, Atmeydanı Sok 46, Sultanahmet
🍴 Café in the courtyard
🕐 Tue–Sun 9–4:30 🚇 Sultanahmet
💷 Inexpensive

7 Yerebatan Sarayı (Basilica Cistern)

Often known as the Sunken Palace, this vast, cathedral-like, underground chamber was built in AD532 by Emperor Justinian to store water for the city (it was carried from Belgrade Forest, 14km (9 miles) north of the city on the Valens Viaduct). The cistern, 140m (460 feet) long and 70m (230 feet) wide, reveals a great deal about Byzantine technical sophistica-tion. Its huge domed ceiling is supported by 336 marble columns; two at the very back rest on enormous marble Medusa heads that were taken from an ancient site in Asia Minor. During Ottoman rule, the cistern was used to supply water to Topkapı Palace but fell into disuse in the 15th century. Restoration work began in the late 1980s. Today, only a shallow depth of water remains, which supports a population of fish and acts as a wishing well for visitors. A walk-way above keeps your feet dry and there's a small café inside where you can enjoy a drink by candlelight.

🕇 179 C2 ✉ Yerebatan Caddesi, Sultanahmet 🕐 Daily 9–4:30 🍴 Café (£) 🚇 Sultanahmet 💷 Moderate

8 Mısır Çarşısı (Egyptian Bazaar)

The place to come for real Turkish delight (*lokum*), the Egyptian (or Spice) Bazaar sells all manner of treats for the sweet-toothed, as well as spices by the kilo and reputedly the most potent aphrodisiacs in Turkey.

One of two marble sculptures of Medusa, brought from Asia Minor by the Byzantines for use in Yerebatan Sarayı

The U-shaped bazaar – which got its name because taxes levied in Egypt were used to fund its construction – has a distinctive character, with shopkeepers constantly thrusting silver platters of *lokum* under your nose, exhorting you to try a selection before you buy. Each vendor has a tantalising display, be it sweets, spices, olives or honey, and you can buy Turkish pastrami (*pastourma*) by the slice. Prices don't vary much between vendors but are higher than in the surrounding back streets.

One of Istanbul's most renowned restaurants, Pandeli, is located on the upper floor of the bazaar, above the eastern gate-way nearest the waterfront. Here you can try traditional Greek-influenced cuisine at reasonable prices and watch the hustle and bustle in the arcades below.

🕇 179 C3 ✉ Eminönü, at the south-west corner of the Yeni Camii
🕐 Mon–Sat 8:30–6:30 🚇 Eminönü
⛴ Eminönü 💷 Free

Turkish delight on sale in Mısır Çarşısı

supporting columns, juxtaposing open space with structural elements, came to represent pure Islamic form. The interior is exceptionally light because of its many windows and muted decoration.

The mosque sits at the centre of a huge complex surrounded by five *medreses* (Islamic schools), a library, *hamam* (Turkish bath), *kervansary* (caravanserai) and public kitchen to feed the poor, all of which became standard features of large imperial mosques throughout the Ottoman Empire.

In a small cemetery to the right of the mosque you'll find the tombs of Süleyman, the most powerful man in the world during his lifetime, and of his wife Roxelana, both elaborately carved from marble and decorated with fine İznik tiles (➤ panel, page 45).

➕ 179 B3 ✉ Sıddık Samı, off Süleymaniye Caddesi
🕐 At all times except prayer times (➤ Top tips, page 45)
🎟 Free

🔟 Kariye Camii (Church of St Saviour in Chora)

The late-Byzantine religious mosaics and frescoes in this simple 14th-century chapel (now a museum) are exceptional.

The mosaics, commissioned by the church's patron, the scholar and theologian Theodore Metochites, were not destroyed when the church was converted to a mosque in 1511. Depicting Christ, the saints and scenes from the Bible, the mosaics are set apart by the figures' realistic facial expressions and their sense of physical action. The mosaics swathe the upper walls and cupolas of both the outer and inner narthexes of the church, though the walls of

�ⅼ Süleymaniye Camii (Süleymaniye Mosque)

Considered to be the finest example of Ottoman religious architecture in the world, the Süleymaniye complex was designed for Süleyman the Magnificent by his chief architect Sinan and completed in 1557 when the empire was enjoying its golden age.

Sinan aimed to surpass the Byzantine form of Aya Sofya, and Süleymaniye's prayer room, a perfect square, and it's dome, the diameter of which is half its height, show his passion for symmetry. Its structure of open prayer room and minimal

The 16th-century mosaics in the narthex of Kariye Camii depict the lives of Christ and the Virgin Mary

the nave are lined with marble so few images survive in this part of the church.

The frescoes can be found to the right of the nave, in the *parecclesion* (funerary chapel) of Theodore Metochites. Depicting the Last Judgement and the Harrowing of Hell, they, too, exude realism and vigour, aided by their exceptionally strong colour. The finest example is a graphic illustration of Christ's resurrection.

✚ 178 A4 ✉ Kariye Bostana Sok, Fener district ⏰ Thu–Mon 9–4:30 🍴 Café outside the church (£) 🎫 Moderate

The 14th-century Galata Kulesi stands proud above the waterfront

🕦 Boat Trip on the Bosphorus

If you want to escape the noisy, dusty city streets, take to the water for a glimpse of the 19th-century palaces and traditional *yolu* (wooden mansions) that occupy shoreside positions in the genteel northern suburbs of Istanbul.

In summer, arrive early to get a good seat on the motor boat (some can carry about 200 people so they might get crowded). Heading out along the west bank you'll pass the extensive white marble façade of Dolmabahçe Palace (➤ 55), then the

Çırağan Palace – now a splendid hotel – before you sail under the Bosphorus Bridge. Inaugurated in 1973, this was the first bridge to span the waterway separating Europe from Asia.

Choose between a full-day cruise with lunch included or a four-hour trip that reaches the large castle of Rumeli Hisarı before turning back along the eastern bank towards the city. There are no grand palaces here but you'll see several *yolu*; some have been refurbished by affluent Istanbul citizens, but others are in need of a little attention.

✚ 179 C3 ✉ Dock three, Eminönü ferry docks ⏰ Daily approx 10:30, 1:30 🚇 Eminönü ⛴ (Ferry) Eminönü 🎫 Expensive

🕦 Galata Kulesi (Galata Tower)

This simple 14th-century watch-tower, set on a small hill, offers fantastic 360-degree views over historic Istanbul, the waterways of the Bosphorus and the modern city.

Built by the Genoese, it was used as a prison by the Ottomans but today its upper floor, 70m (230 feet) above the ground, houses a restaurant reached via an elevator. The panoramic platform is narrow and perhaps not for those who suffer from vertigo, but take your camera to capture the minarets of Aya Sofya, Sultanahmet and Süleymaniye mosques, and your binoculars to glimpse daily life in the streets of the Galata district below. It's a busy neighbourhood where women sit cross-legged on roof-top terraces, crocheting and drinking tea, old men gather on benches at street corners and lines of washing hang between old apartment buildings like canopies of bunting.

✚ 178 C4 ✉ Galata Kulesi Sok, Galata district ⏰ Daily 9–5 for general tourist visits. Reopens as a restaurant in the evenings 🚇 Karaköy, Beyoğlu/Taksim 🎫 Moderate

🕦 Beyoğlu

Western influences are most evident in the Beyoğlu district of the city, a once seedy area that is fast becoming

the most fashionable place in Istanbul to shop and socialise. It's also, aside from Sultanahmet, the main area for tourist hotels, so you're likely to spend at least some time here.

Beyoğlu, which lies across the Golden Horn from old Istanbul, enjoyed its heyday in the 19th century, when European diplomats and bankers built imposing European-style mansions here. This huge foreign population, particularly rich in Greek and Jewish culture, gave the district an atmosphere

Smart boutiques and stylish restaurants line İstiklal Caddesi in the Beyoğlu district

distinct from that of the older parts of Istanbul, which remains today (though foreign residents are far fewer since the establishment of the Turkish Republic in 1923). Beyoğlu's main avenue, İstiklal Caddesi, is traffic-free – except for the regular tram service that runs along it – and lined with modern boutiques, its side streets full of Western-style bars and restaurants. Head for the Çiçek Pasajı (Flower Market), which is particularly renowned for its traditional eateries. Beyoğlu has now melded with neighbouring Galatasaray and Taksim Meydanı, which together constitute the centre of the modern city.

➕ 178 D5 🚉 İstiklal Caddesi

🄬 Dolmabahçe Sarayı (Dolmabahçe Palace)

The vast Dolmabahçe Palace, built for the Ottoman sultans when Topkapı Palace became outdated, and their residence from the mid-19th century, is almost gaudy in its excessive ornamentation. No expense was spared in its construction – it virtually bankrupted the empire – and the result is without doubt spectacular. It was designed in a grand rococo style that was fashionable in Europe at the time. Gold leaf smothers practically every interior surface, set off by solid gold fittings and a profusion of marble and alabaster. Highlights of the tour include the Throne Room, which has a magnificent *trompe l'oeil* ceiling supported by 56 Corinthinan columns, the State Room, where you can see the world's largest chandelier, and the Grand Hall of the Reception of Ambassadors, richly decorated with carved and gilded panels.

Dolmabahçe witnessed the final demise of the Ottoman Empire when the Turkish Republic was declared here in 1923. Perhaps surprisingly, considering his reformist policies, Atatürk made the palace his home after he took power and died here in November 1938.

➕ 178 E5 🖂 Dolmabahçe Caddesi, Beşiktaş district 🕐 Tue, Wed, Fri–Sun 9–4. Guided tours only, departing every half hour; palace: 45 min, harem: 35 min 🚉 Beşiktaş 🚏 Beşiktaş 💷 Expensive; harem: moderate

Further Afield

15 Şile

A pretty clifftop seaside resort on the Black Sea coast, Şile is the place to come to watch Istanbullu at play. Many wealthy families have holiday homes here, and every weekend from May to September there is a stream of traffic heading northeast from Istanbul for the 90-minute journey to the town.

The beaches are a major draw; the fine sand is hemmed in by rocky promontories. At the small fishing port, guarded by a Genoese tower, you can watch the catch being brought ashore. The main street above the port has a number of old mansions, which are now being given a new lease of life as boutiques or restaurants with panoramic views over the coastline.

Şile sees few foreign visitors and perhaps this alone makes it worth a visit. However, accommodation can be difficult to find during high season.

181 E4 Black Sea coast, 70km (44 miles) from Istanbul
From the station near the Üsküdar jetty

Şile, an attractive fishing port on the Black Sea coast, is a popular weekend retreat from Istanbul

16 Safranbolu

Depite being a long way from Istanbul (a visit requires an overnight stop each way), Safranbolu's unique collection of Ottoman domestic architecture makes the journey worthwhile. Set in stunning landscape along a deep ravine, the mansions, or *konak*, are terraced on a hillside and linked by narrow cobbled streets.

The heart of the historic district, Carşı or Eski Safranbolu, was given Unesco World Heritage status in 1994 and is easily explored on foot. Allow a morning to wander off the main thoroughfares and down the side alleys. Although many buildings have been renovated and work continues on others, some of the most interesting houses and streets are those whose patina of age is still intact.

One of the finest mansions, Kaymakamlar Evi, has been converted into a museum providing information about the Ottoman architecture of the town. For panoramic views, make your way to Hıdırlık Park on the hillside above the museum. It looks most attractive in the afternoon when the light plays on the buildings across the ravine.

184 D5 520km (323 miles) east of Istanbul; 220km (137 miles) north of Ankara From Esenlar bus station, Istanbul

Tourist Office

Kazdağioğlu Meydani 1 0372 712 3863; www.safranbolu.gov.tr

Where to... Stay

Prices
Expect to pay for two people sharing a double room
£ under US$130   ££ US$130–US$230   £££ more than US$230

Armada Hotel £

Run with style by Sabahattin Bey
(▶ Balikci Sabahattin, page 58),
Armada is cool and chic but friendly.
It has comfortable (if noisy) rooms,
and a great villagey location, a block
from the sea at Marmara's shore-
level. The attractions of Sultanahmet
await via an uphill stroll through
vibrant backstreets.

➕ 179 C2 ✉ Ahırkapı Sultanahmet 34400 ☎ 0212 455 4455; fax: 0212 455 4499; info@armadahotel.com.tr; www.armadahotel.com.tr

Bonjour Guesthouse £

In a great Sultanahmet location, and
a short walk from the sights,
Bonjour is perhaps the most
charmingly run guesthouse in town.
Rooms are romantic and impeccably
clean and the patio garden is a
perfect spot to take breakfast.

➕ 179 C2 ✉ Mimar Mehmet Ağa Caddesi, Amiral Tafdil Sokak No 10, Sultanahmet ☎ 0212 516 3052; fax: 0212 518 4954; www.bonjour-guesthouse.net

Bosphorus Palace £££

On the Asian side of Istanbul, but
within easy reach of the European
side by ferry, Bosphorus Palace is a
stylish, discreet 14-bedroom hotel in
the former residence of an Ottoman
vizier. With its high ceilings, quality
antique furniture and an unsurpassed waterfront position affording
fine views over the Bosphorous, it is
a good choice for those wishing to
escape Istanbul's hurly-burly.

➕ 178 off E4 ✉ Yalıboyu Caddesi 64, Beylerbeyi 34676 ☎ 0216 422 0003; fax: 0216 422 0012; www.bosphoruspalace.com

The Four Seasons £££

This hotel occupies premises that
used to house political prisoners.
Nowadays, you'll be rubbing shoulders with a well-heeled, international
crowd, attended by impeccably
trained staff. Just a short walk from
Sultanahmet Camii (▶ 44–45) and
Aya Sofya Camii (▶ 42–43), the
Four Seasons offers the unusual city
luxury of calm in its 65 rooms, all of
which overlook a pretty courtyard.

➕ 179 C2 ✉ Tevkifhane Sokak 1, Sultanahmet 34110 ☎ 0212 638 8200; fax: 0212 638 8210; www.fourseasons.com ⊙ All year

Nomade Hotel £

Sensitively run by English-speaking
twin sisters, Nomade deserves its
loyal clientele, who return for its
clean rooms with private bathrooms
and *kilim*-hung lobby. This firm
favourite has reinvented itself with
a fantastic contemporary makeover
in 2006. The twins love to impart
their wealth of local knowledge
to their guests.

➕ 179 C2 ✉ Divanyolu, Ticarethane Sokak 15, Sultanahmet 34400 ☎ 0212 513 8172; fax: 0212 513 2404; www.hotelnomade.com

Sirkeci Konak ££

Overlooking Gülhane Park close to
the waterfront below Sultanahmet,
this historic konak (mansion) has
been beautifully renovated, with 52
delightful luxurious and spacious
rooms along with a pool and
panoramic restaurant. There's a
small indoor swimming pool,
sauna, gym and Turkish bath on
the premises.

➕ 179 C3 ✉ Taya Hatun Sokak 5, Sirkeci 34120 ☎ 0212 528 4344; fax: 0212 528 4455; www.sirkecikonak.com

Where to...
Eat and Drink

Prices

Expect to pay for a three-course meal, excluding drinks
£ under US$15   ££ US$15–US$25   £££ more than US$25

Balıkcı Sabahattin £££

Under the same ownership as the Armada Hotel (▶ 57), this lively fish restaurant inhabits an Ottoman house in winter, spilling out into the adjoining alley in spring and summer. Top choices are the excellent tray-service *mezze*, incomparably fresh fish and wonderful *midye pilaf* (mussel rice) studded with tiny currants. It's an atmospheric place, popular with Istanbul's stylish crowd. Advance reservations are essential.

🚻 179 C2 ✉ Cankurtaran, Sultanahmet ☎ 0212 458 1824
🕐 Daily 12–3, 6–1

Cezayir £££

Since 2005, Cezayir has been creating a stir with the young and trendy crowd of Istanbul, and the chic contemporary décor is matched by the menu, which presents a mixture of western fusion and Turkish dishes. If you don't want a full meal, try a couple of *mezze*, have a drink at the spacious bar or alternatively relax over tea or coffee in the pleasant gardens.

🚻 178 C5 ✉ Hayriye Caddesi 12, Galatasaray, 34425 ☎ 0212 245 4892; www.cezayir-istanbul.com
🕐 Daily 9am–2am

Dârrüziyâfe ££

An unusually happy marriage of ancient monument and modern attitude, Dârrüziyâfe's historic surroundings contrast cleverly with a contemporary, pared-down take on classic Ottoman food. Hot and cold *mezze* are on offer – *mança* (spinach with yoghurt) is especially fresh, creamy and sharp. Dârrüziyâfe is also justly famous for its *tavuklu kolboregi* (spicy chicken in pastry).

🚻 179 B3 ✉ Şifahane Caddesi, in the Süleymaniye Camii complex (▶ 53) ☎ 0212 511 8414 🕐 Daily; closed lunch and some evenings during Ramadan

Haci Abdullah ££

This restaurant has been serving archetypal Ottoman cuisine since the time of the Ottoman Empire, opening its door in 1888. It's moved with the times however, being thoroughly renovated at the start of the decade, and it is also the proud recipient of the internationally recognised ISO 9000 Quality Certificate. An excellent range of salads, grilled meats and pastries, in fact every staple of Turkish cuisine, is served here. However, alcohol is not available.

🚻 178 D5 ✉ Ad'a Camii Yanı Sakızad'acı Caddesi 17, Beyod'lu ☎ 0212 293 8561; www.haciabdullah.com.tr
🕐 Daily 11am–10pm

Pâtisserie de Pera £££

You can marvel at the view over the Golden Horn from this old-style pâtisserie. It's part of the Pera Palas Hotel, which was built to accommodate travellers from the Orient Express. In keeping with its history, pastries are in the grand European style, although Turkish classics such as *kadayif* (shredded wheat in honey syrup) also make an appearance.

🚻 178 C5 ✉ Meşrutiyet Caddesi No 89/100, Harbiye ☎ 0212 251 4560; fax: 0212 251 4089
🕐 Daily 8:30–6:30

Where to...
Shop

Istanbul built its reputation as a shopping city during the Ottoman era, when the most skillful artisans in the empire handled fine Asian and African raw materials such as gold, silk, gemstones, brass and copper. Today, Istanbul is still Turkey's best place to shop for native handicrafts.

OLD ISTANBUL

At the top of the range, the **gold jewellery** in the **Kapalıçarşı** (Grand Bazaar, ▶ 49–50), mostly 18 and 22 carat, is outstanding. Precious metals are sold by weight at the day's price, with very little added for the workmanship involved in creating the piece. This makes ornate jewellery very good value. Precious stones can be inserted into the setting of your choice. You'll find that rings can be sized overnight, so you won't have to wait long for your purchase. Chains and bracelets are sold by weight, but jewellery set with stones is not. **Silver** is also used in jewellery, as well as cutlery, tea sets, napkin rings and picture frames, all sold by weight. Many arcades are devoted to selling **carpets**, ranging from exquisite silk rugs to flat-weave *kilims*.

There is also an excellent range of more affordable souvenirs, including hand-worked Islamic handicrafts. Carved latticework **coffee tables** with copper tops could grace a living room or conservatory. Most fold away (they were originally made to be carried by nomadic Islamic peoples) and are easy to carry home. *Tavla* (backgammon) boards and chess sets inlaid with different coloured woods are good value for money. *Hookah* pipes are an almost obligatory kitsch purchase, along with **Meershaum pipes**, carved from soft white Meershaum stone. Multicoloured textiles also catch the eye – from vibrant Turkish slippers to woven throws, or the traditional patterns and colours of Iznik tiles found on a whole range of ceramics.

Sahaflar Çarşısı, the small secondhand **book market** just off Beyazıt Meydanı, to the west of the Grand Bazaar, is worth a visit. It sells more modern books than old ones and the English editions are expensive, but it's still a good place to browse.

Divan Yolu Caddesi, the main arterial route through the Beyazıt district, has some excellent but expensive carpet shops and the small side streets leading off here host a plethora of small shops where you can buy handicrafts of all kinds.

And don't forget the **Mısır Çarşısı** (Egyptian Bazaar, ▶ 52) for Turkish delight and other edibles.

Of course Turkey is famed for copies of these same products sold at a fraction of the price – you can get fake designer goods on the streets surrounding the Grand Bazaar, but you must make up your own mind about the quality of the goods – some are excellent, others dubious.

NEW ISTANBUL

The modern city offers a total contrast. The fashion industry is buoyant, spurred on by designers such as Rıfat Özbek. You'll find all the international names in clothing and style products at prices favourable to those at home. **İstiklal Caddesi**, in the Beyoğlu district (▶ 54–55), forms the heart of 21st-century Istanbul, with many smart fashionable boutiques.

The city has over 40 shopping malls with the most plush, **Cevahir Mall**, being one of the largest in Europe.

Where to...
Be Entertained

Istanbul offers the best entertainment in Turkey and arguably in the Eastern Mediterranean. In addition to a lively night scene, numerous culture and arts festivals fill the calendar. The tourist office on the corner of the Hipodrom in Sultanahmet (Meydani) provides details of what's on.

BELLY DANCING

Belly dancers in smoky nightclubs are an enduring image of Turkey, and it's worth seeing a show while you're in Istanbul. **Istanbulin** is a new dinner and show venue (Cumhuriyet Caddesi, Cebel Topu Sokak 2, Harbiye, tel: 0212 291 8440, www.istanbulin.com) where the dancing combines traditional Turkish performances with Western cabaret style. Book ahead for a show and dinner. Alternatively, you can have dinner and watch folkloric performances at **Orient House** (Tiyatro Caddesi 27, Eminönü, tel: 0212 517 6163; www.orienthouseistanbul.com).

NIGHTLIFE

You can stay out all night at numerous nightclubs and bars then have breakfast at one of the 24-hour soup shops catering for early morning workers around the markets. **Havana** (Muallim Naci Caddesi 120, Ortaköy, tel: 0212 260 1899) is the latest place to be seen – a vast open arena surrounded by eateries. **Gramafon** (Tünel Meydani 3, Tünel, tel: 0212 293 0786) has long been Istanbul's premier jazz venue and it hosts both international and local musicians at weekends. For more Western-style music and karaoke, the **Gossip Bar** in the Hyatt Regency Hotel (Taskilasla Caddesi, Taksim, tel: 0212 368 1234) offers live music, video screens and karaoke. **Laila** (Muallim Naci Caddesi, Ortakoy, tel: 0212 256 9016) is a nightclub complex with a capacity for 3,000 and several restaurants, while **Roxy** (Arslanyatagi Sok 9, Siraselviler Caddesi, Taksim, tel: 0212 245 6539) has themed nights, including techno and 1970s.

Dulcinea (Meselik Sok 20, Istiklal Caddesi, Beyoğlu, tel: 0212 245 1071, closed July–August) is the hottest and the most expensive nightspot/bar/eatery in the city with a bent towards electronic sounds. This is the place for the glitterati to meet and be seen.

Early in the evening (around 9pm), young, less affluent Istanbullu head to **Babylon** (Şeyh Bender Sok, Asmalimescit, Tünel, Beyoğlu, tel: 0212 292 7368, www.babylon.com), with its mix of pop, reggae and Turkish avant-garde jazz. Babylon closes early – at midnight – so you can then pick your venue for late-night revelry.

FESTIVALS

The summer is full of cultural events organised by the Istanbul Culture and Art Foundation (www.iksv.com). The **International Istanbul Film Festival** kicks off in early April, where the Golden Tulip award is presented to best film. This is followed by the **Theatre Festival** (May–June), the **Music Festival** (June), and finally the **International Istanbul Jazz Festival** in July or early August.

For the last 20 years, on odd years, the city has held an arts **Biennial** (from mid-September to early November), drawing strands from all genres, and staged at a variety of venues across the city.

North Aegean

ΑΥΤΟΚΡΑΤΟ
ΤΟΥ ΚΡΑ

Getting Your Bearings

With only one major international holiday resort, the Northern Aegean seems at first to have fewer attractions than other parts of the Turkish coast, but you'll be amply rewarded if you're willing to explore. The area's archaeological remains are some of the best in Turkey and rural life abounds, so, although you'll need a rental car to cover the long distances involved, your journey will never be dull.

The south is the most developed part of this region. İzmir (ancient Smyrna) on the coast is the third largest conurbation in Turkey and a thriving industrial port with an interesting old quarter, good museums and excellent bazaar. Çeşme, 80km (50 miles) west, at the end of a breezy peninsula, is the premier resort of the Northern Aegean, the place for sailing, watersports and spa treatments.

Central Northern Aegean sits on a wide coastal plain with some good beaches and modest holiday resorts favoured by Turkish families. Here too are the larger resorts of Ayvalık and Foça. One outstanding ancient site rises from the endless cotton fields – the majestic acropolis of Pergamum, capital of western Turkey during Roman times.

Page 61: Detail from the façade of the Imperial Hall, Sart

Above: A farmer sells his produce at Ayvalık market

Below: The harbour at Foça

The very north of the region is a day's drive from İzmir, but worth the effort for its dramatic peaks and verdant pine forests, traditional Turkish lifestyle and scattering of ancient sites (such as the famous city of Troy). Base yourself at tiny, bohemian, Behramkale or unpretentious Çanakkale, from where a short ferry ride north across the Dardanelle Straight leads to the World War I graveyards at Gallipoli.

★ Don't Miss

1. **Sart (Sardis)** ➤ 66
2. **Pergamum** ➤ 68
3. **Çeşme** ➤ 70

At Your Leisure

4. İzmir ➤ 72
5. Foça ➤ 72
6. Ayvalık ➤ 73
7. Assos ➤ 73
8. Truva (Troy) ➤ 74
9. Gelibolu Milliparkı (Gallipoli National Park) ➤ 74

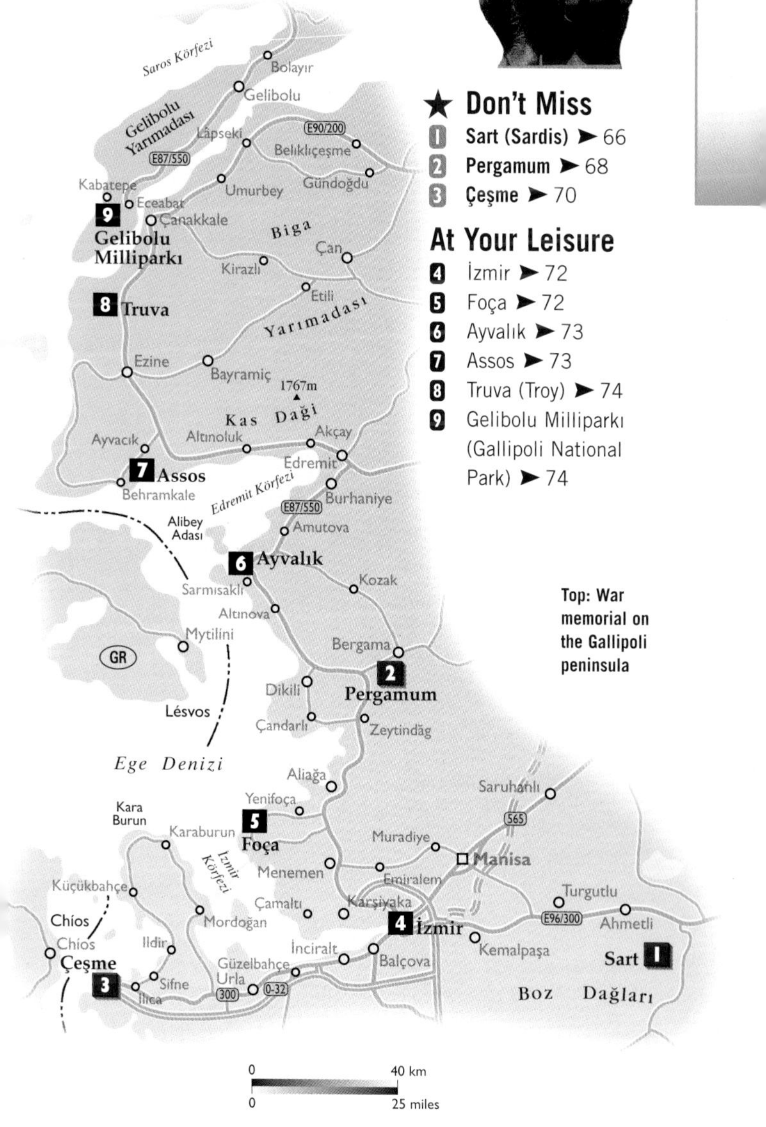

Top: War memorial on the Gallipoli peninsula

Saros Körfezi

Bolayır
Gelibolu
Gelibolu Yarımadası
Kapseki
E90/200
Beliklçeşme
E87/550
Umurbey
Gündoğdu
Kabatepe
Eceabat
9 Çanakkale
Gelibolu Milliparkı
Biga
Çan
Kirazlı
Etili
8 Truva
Yarımadası
Ezine
Bayramiç
1767m
Kas Dağı
Ayvacık
Altınoluk
Akçay
7 Assos
Edremit
Behramkale
Edremit Körfezi
E87/550
Burhaniye
Alibey Adası
Amutova
6 Ayvalık
Sarmısaklı
Kozak
Altınova
Mytilini
GR
Bergama
Dikili
2 Pergamum
Çandarlı
Zeytindağ
Lésvos

Ege Denizi

Aliağa
Saruhanlı
Kara Burun
Yenifoça
565
Karaburun
5 Foça
Muradiye
Manisa
Menemen
Emiralem
Turgutlu
Küçükbahçe
Çamaltı
Karşiyaka
E96/300
Ahmetli
Chios
Mordoğan
İnciralt
4 İzmir
Chios
İldir
Güzelbahçe
Kemalpaşa
Sart 1
Çeşme 3
Urla
300
0-32
Balçova
Boz Dağları
Sifne
Ilıca

0 — 40 km
0 — 25 miles

İzmir is a good centre for reaching Pergamum and Sart (Sardis) before you spend a couple of nights at Çeşme. Otherwise, base yourself at Çanakkale on the Dardanelles if you intend to visit the war graves at Gelibolu (Gallipoli) and the ancient sites of Troy and Assos. Be prepared: the further north you go, the fewer specialised facilities are available for tourists and there's less accommodation, so you'll have to do a lot of driving.

The North Aegean in Four Days

Day 1

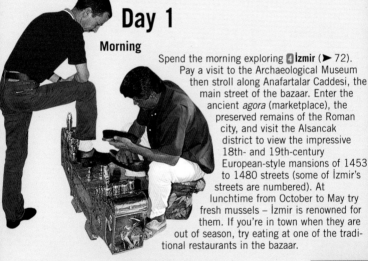

Morning

Spend the morning exploring ⁴ İzmir (► 72). Pay a visit to the Archaeological Museum then stroll along Anafartalar Caddesi, the main street of the bazaar. Enter the ancient *agora* (marketplace), the preserved remains of the Roman city, and visit the Alsancak district to view the impressive 18th- and 19th-century European-style mansions of 1453 to 1480 streets (some of İzmir's streets are numbered). At lunchtime from October to May try fresh mussels – İzmir is renowned for them. If you're in town when they are out of season, try eating at one of the traditional restaurants in the bazaar.

Afternoon

Make your way to ❶ Sart (► 66–67), to visit the ancient city of Sardis, home of the legendary King Croesus. Here you can see the remains of two magnificent buildings, the Imperial Hall and the Temple of Artemis.

Evening

Return to İzmir and stroll with the locals along the Kordon waterfront promenade in the Alsancak district or, if you feel too jaded after your long day, take a carriage ride along the route instead. You'll also find numerous restaurants and bars here.

Day 2

Morning
From İzmir, set out early for **2 Pergamum** (► 68–69), 93km (58 miles) north along the E87/550 then inland on the 240. This ancient city (left and below) has two sites, separated by the modern city of Bergama and its fascinating old town, warranting a full morning's exploration.

Afternoon/Evening
Make your way back south to **5 Foça** (► 72–73), on the 250 coast road, where there is a choice of restaurants in the picturesque harbour. Stay overnight here.

Day 3

Morning/Afternoon
Travel west from Foça to **3 Çeşme** (► 70–71). Visit the castle, then spend the rest of the afternoon exploring the town before heading to the harbour to book a *gület* ride for tomorrow – there'll be many ticket touts vying for business. A trip to Donkey Island (► Top tips, page 71) – inhabited only by the eponymous beasts of burden – is a good choice.

Day 4

This is a day for pure relaxation, floating along on board a *gület* in the sunshine and enjoying the kind of views that are difficult to see from a car. You'll depart around 10:30am and be back in the harbour by 4:30pm. Don't forget your swimming costume, suncream and snorkel!

⓪ **Sart** (Sardis)

Two outstanding monuments put ancient Sardis on the modern tourist map. The town's Roman gymnasium and baths complex displays a spectacular renovated façade, while its Hellenistic temple was the largest in the Greek world at the time of its construction.

Sardis was founded about 5,000 years ago and grew rich on a prodigious gold seam in the nearby River Pactolus. It was capital of the region during Lydian times (► 16) and one of its rulers, King Croesus (ruled *c*560–546BC), became the richest man in the world from the proceeds of gold smelting. It might be hard to imagine the city's former glory today, but what you can see of the partially excavated site is in surprisingly good condition.

The **Roman gymnasium** sits in the centre of the modern village of Sart. From the car park, follow the path on the far right of the remains, nearest the modern road, where you can walk beside a partially **reconstructed marble street**, 18m (20 yards) wide and flanked with Byzantine shops. This was the heart of ancient Sardis. One section has been completely cleared to show the cart tracks that are worn into its surface. Turn left at the remains of the 3rd-century synagogue into an immense open courtyard. From here, you can take in the full majesty of the front façade of the **Imperial Hall**, entry to the complex of baths and sports halls, restored to its original 3rd-century design. The two-storey brick and marble wall is a masterful example of symmetrical design and is decorated with marble friezes and intricately carved columns. Unfortunately, much of the complex beyond lies in ruins.

The **Temple of Artemis** lies 1km (0.5 miles) from the gymnasium (the turning is signposted on the right, as you approach from Izmir, before you reach the sports complex). If you don't feel up to walking between the two, it is possible to drive to the temple (► Top tips, page 67).

Detail from the façade of the Imperial Hall

A Golden Age

In ancient times, sheeps' fleeces were immersed in the river until minute specks of gold were trapped in their fine hairs. The wool was then dried and brushed to retrieve the precious metal. Historians have suggested that the Greek myth of the Golden Fleece was inspired by the practice.

The temple, which was larger than the Parthenon in Athens, was built in the 6th century BC, on the site of an earlier structure. An earthquake in AD17 badly damaged the temple, and when excavations started in 1910 only the tops of two columns were visible. However, the remaining temple platform and handful of standing columns visible today suggest the size and beauty of the original edifice, and this combined with the idyllic setting, surrounded by magnificent russet-coloured peaks, make a visit more than worthwhile.

🔲 182 C4
✉ 97km (60 miles) east of İzmir, on the E96/E881 road
🕐 Daily 8:30–5:30
🚌 To Sart from İzmir
🎫 Gymnasium: inexpensive; Temple of Artemis: inexpensive

The Midas Touch

In Greek mythology, Sardis's riches came from King Midas. He wished to have everything he touched turn to gold but when he discovered he could neither eat nor drink, he pleaded with the gods to release him from the curse. Washing his hands in the River Pactolus, he released the gold into the waters.

Below left: The towering columns and archways of the Imperial Hall
Below: Mosaics in the 3rd-century synagogue

SART: INSIDE INFO

Top tips The frieze of the Roman gymnasium is **best viewed in the morning.**

In more depth Sardis was first excavated in the early years of the 20th century by Howard Crosby Butler for Princeton University in the US. Butler was a legendary archaeologist who was credited with having stopped an insurrection of local Ottoman Turks while at the site, armed only with a stick of bamboo. Many of the artefacts he uncovered are on display in the Metropolitan Museum of Art in New York.

2 Pergamum

At the height of its power Pergamum rivalled Egypt's Alexandria in prestige. The city, renowned for its medical treatments, was adorned with splendid temples and public buildings. Following excavations in the 19th century, the best parts of ancient Pergamum are now in the Pergamum Museum in Berlin, but though stripped of its finest decorations, the city's stunning location and marvellous theatre are more than adequate compensation.

Founded in 301BC, Pergamum represented the first Roman footfall across the Aegean Sea. The city became the capital of the Roman province of Asia in 133BC, but its heyday was shortlived and it had started to decline by the 2nd century AD. What's left of the ancient city now exists as two main archaeological sites, the **Acropolis** ("upper city") and, 7km (4 miles) away on the other side of modern Bergama, the **Asklepeion**, the ancient centre of healing.

The Acropolis

Built on a 280m (920-foot) outcrop, Pergamum's Acropolis has a truly breathtaking setting with panoramic views down the valley and out towards the Aegean.

The best place to get an overview of the ancient city itself is from the small, square tower-like structure that stands on the far side of the scant remains of the **Sanctuary of Athena** (take the first left after the ticket office). From here, you can see the **Roman theatre**, a spectacular piece of engineering, cascading down the steep hillside below. It retains its original Hellenistic design, lacking a stage wall and though the 78 rows of seating are not well preserved, the sheer drop makes exploring the theatre an exhilarating experience.

From the top of the theatre, your eye is drawn to the temple plateau above, which rests on an immense vaulted platform (the path to the theatre winds through these vaults). At its centre, the monumental 2nd-century **Temple of Trajan** is surrounded by a stately *temenos* (ceremonial walkway). The eastern corner columns and pediment of the temple's inner sanctum have been re-erected, suggesting some of the site's former glory.

The Asklepeion

This ancient health complex was state-of-the-art during the Roman era, with celebrity Romans clamouring for treatment. Its reputation sprang mainly from the fame of the influential physician Galen, who was born in Pergamum.

From the ticket office, the western section of **Via Tecta**, a marble-colonnaded road, leads to the ceremonial courtyard of the sanctuary. Beyond, there's an open square and two round temples lie to your left. The furthest one, dedicated to the deity Telesphorus, known for his healing powers, can be reached either by footpath or through an underground tunnel from the centre of the square. This round two-storey temple was a diagnosis and treatment unit with aromatic steam rooms to induce dreaming (on which diagnosis was based).

To give a glimpse of its former glory, parts of the Temple of Trajan have been re-erected

TAKING A BREAK

Meydan Restaurant (Izmir Caddesi 163) offers tasty kebaps and other Turkish staples but is well known in the city for it's excellent home-made moussaka made fresh each day. Supplies are limited so choose your table early.

➕ 180 B1 ⊠ 93km (58 miles) north of İzmir 🚌 From İzmir and Ayvalık

Tourist Office
⊠ Bergama Hükümet Konad'ı, B Blok Zemin Kat ☎ 0232 631 2851

Acropolis
⊠ Kale Yolu, signposted 5km (3 miles) above the town
🕐 Tue–Sun 8:30–5:30 💲 Moderate

Asklepeion
⊠ Asklepeion Caddesi signposted 1km (0.5 miles) south of the town, right off the main road as you leave town, then 1km (0.5 miles) to the site
🕐 Tue–Sun 8:30–5:30 💲 Moderate

PERGAMUM: INSIDE INFO

Top tips Set aside **three hours** to see both the Acropolis and the Asklepeion. As the sites are comparatively far apart, consider taking an organised tour. Otherwise, visit the Acropolis first and take a taxi to the Asklepeion.

• Keep your **camera** pointed at the Asklepeion – not at the military camp nearby.

In more depth Located at the foot of the Acropolis, the interesting old town of **Bergama**, with its twisting cobbled lanes and 2nd-century Roman temple, is also filled with timber-framed Ottoman mansions. The archaeological museum (Arkeoloji Müzesi) on the main street, Bankalar Caddesi, has a collection of finds that remained in Turkey after the German archaeologists had left. There's also a model of the ornate Temple of Zeus; the original was removed from the Acropolis and re-erected in Berlin.

3 Çeşme

The imposing 14th-century Genoese fortress dominates Çeşme's harbour

On the westernmost tip of a large peninsula, Çeşme is a pretty spa resort set around a sturdy Genoese castle and Ottoman *kervansary*. Although the *ymbat* breeze blowing down the Aegean makes the town cooler than many Turkish resorts, it's popular with package tourists and Turkish visitors alike. A berth here allows easy access to the numerous coves and bays of the peninsula, and to the Greek island of Chíos lying just offshore. It's also a great place for windsurfing.

Healing Waters

The Çeşme peninsula sports some of the finest hotels along the coast, thanks mainly to therapeutic hot springs rising from deep underground. Resorts such as **Ilıca** and **Şifne** outside of Çeşme provide traditional treatments for diseases such as rheumatism in addition to luxury European-style spa complexes; they also have long sandy beaches to enjoy. Çeşme means "drinking fountain" and, true to its name, there are more than a dozen **Seljuk and Ottoman fountains** in the streets of the old town, though most have fallen into disrepair with the advent of modern domestic plumbing.

The Sites

The 14th-century **Genoese fortress**, which was extended and refurbished by the Ottomans, is the best, as well as being the most obvious, of Çeşme's Islamic and Byzantine buildings. Unusually, and not very wisely, the fortress was built on the hill behind the seafront, with its western terraces some 10m (33 feet) above the eastern ones, making it easy for enemies to shoot cannonballs into the heart of the stronghold. Inside, a small archaeological museum displays finds dating from prehistory up to the Ottoman era.

To the left as you leave the the fortress is the 16th-century *kervansary*, created by Süleyman the Magnificent for travellers going to Chíos – appropriately now a hotel. Take a look in the verdant courtyard, which is typically Ottoman in design: an open central square with strong, plain outer walls. The lower floors are plainer but support an ornate first-floor stone arcade, off which were rooms for guests.

The Greek Connection

The town's main shopping street **İnkilap Caddesi** runs inland from the castle (right from the castle entrance as you're facing the sea) and leads past souvenir shops and cafés to the plain fortress-like façade of the Greek basilica of **Ayios Haralambos**, an occasional cultural and arts centre. The town had a large Greek population and took a long time to recover from the population exchanges of the 1920s (► 17).

Unique Edibles

The Çeşme peninsula is the only place in Turkey where mastic (*sakyz* in Turkish) is harvested. An aromatic resin scraped from the bark of the mastic tree, it was prized in the Ottoman era as a breath freshener. Local growers now produce mastic jam from the fruit and also mastic *rakı* by infusing the resin in ordinary *rakı*.

TAKING A BREAK

Agrylia Café on the main street in Alacatı resort area is open from the early morning till late at night. The restaurant serves a combination of Turkish and International food.

⊞ 182 A4 ⊠ 80km (50 miles) west from İzmir
🚌 From İzmir

Tourist Office
⊠ İskele Meydanı No 8 on the harbourfront ☎ 0232 712 6653

Çeşme Fortress
⊠ On the seafront 🕒 Tue–Sun 8:30–11:45, 1–5:15
💲 Inexpensive

ÇEŞME: INSIDE INFO

Top tips Visit Çeşme during the week, as weekends see an invasion of visitors from İzmir.

• In the summer, you can take a ferry to the Greek island of **Chíos**, just 10km (6 miles) offshore, or a boat trip to **Donkey Island**, a national park inhabited by the progeny of domestic animals abandoned here when tourism took over from farming. It's best to book your ticket from a vendor in the harbour the day before you want to travel. Most boats leave at 10:30am; allow 6 hours for the trip (May–September daily; April and October trips according to demand).

In more depth Nearby **Alaçatı** has mastic orchards, Seljuk fountains and Greek mansions to visit.

At Your Leisure

4 İzmir

If you're not a city person, İzmir isn't for you. The third-largest urban area in Turkey, it's noisy, dusty and seemingly endless, its suburbs a mass of monochrome concrete apartment blocks. However, there are charms to be found here, and a great legacy – because İzmir, once the Greek city of Smyrna, was for many centuries a thriving hub on the Silk Route from China, and an important commercial port from the 18th and 19th centuries onwards. When the Greek population left in 1922 (▶ 17), the Turkish army set fire to much of the city but a few handsome mansions in the Alsancak district survived.

The compact area around Konak Square has many of the city's attractions including an archaeological museum, an interesting ethnographic museum concentrating on the Ottomans and an elaborate clock tower, presented to the city by the sultan in 1901. Inland, through the bazaar, is the Roman *agora*, a marketplace featuring a Corinthian column.

To experience the city's essence, take a stroll or a ride in a horse-drawn carriage along the Kordon (the seafront boulevard), where locals come to take the cool air.

✚ 182 B4 🚌 Connections from major towns and cities ✈ From Istanbul/Antalya

Tourist Office
🖂 Akdeniz Mah, 1344 Sokak, No 2
☎ 0232 445 7390

Archaeological Museum
🖂 Bahri Baba Parki (Bahri Baba Park)
🕐 Tue–Sun 8:30–5:30
▯ Inexpensive

Ethnographic Museum
🖂 Bahri Baba Parki (Bahri Baba Park)
🕐 Tue–Sun 8:30–5:30
▯ Inexpensive

The ornate clock tower in İzmir's Konak Square

Agora
🖂 816 Sokak 🕐 Tue–Sun 8:30–noon, 1–5 ▯ Inexpensive

5 Foça

A wonderful place to stop for lunch, or a little longer, Foça is a fishing village-turned-resort that has not yet lost its charm. An imposing Genoese fortress dominates the seafront, between the two harbours. The northern Küçükdeniz is the more picturesque of the two, and is the centre of seafront dining and after-dark action. The old town has a network of narrow cobbled streets –

Going to Greece
If you decide to visit a Greek island, travel agents will ask you to leave your passport or a photocopy of your passport with them overnight before you depart. Don't be alarmed: it's easier for them to complete the necessary paperwork for the customs and immigration service after the agency is closed. They will give your passport back the following morning so you'll have it when you enter Greece.

many of which are traffic-free – with some pretty whitewashed fishermen's houses and a small number of Ottoman mansions. Though it sees foreign holidaymakers, Foça is also popular with weekenders from nearby İzmir, so you'll be among Turks relaxing and enjoying themselves.

🚏 182 B5 ✉ 70km (44 miles) north-west of İzmir 🚌 From İzmir

Tourist Office
✉ Atatürk Blvd, Foça Girisi No 1, just north of the central square ☎ 0232 812 5534

6 Ayvalık
The largest resort in the northern Aegean, Ayvalık retains much of the atmosphere of an authentic Turkish fishing town. Until the 1920s' separation, most of the town's population was Greek, and in its back streets

you can see once-fine Hellenic mansions that now house shops and businesses. Thursday is market day, when people from the outlying areas bring their produce to town and the already narrow thoroughfares are filled with vendors selling items of every kind.

You can take a boat trip from the seafront to the Greek island of Lésvos (Lesbos). You'll need to book it the day before and leave your passport overnight with the travel agent (see panel).

🚏 180 B1 ✉ 157km (98 miles) north of İzmir 🚌 From İzmir and Çanakkale

Tourist Office
✉ Yat Limani Carşışı (opposite the harbour) ☎ 0266 312 2122

7 Assos
For the stark beauty of its location, the ancient city of Assos is hard to beat. Built during the 8th century BC on the pinnacle of a solid granite outcrop, it was protected during Byzantine times by a stone wall more than 15m (50 feet) high and 3km (2 miles) long, the remains of which still form an imposing barrier.
The crowning glory of Assos is the Temple of Athena, which was erected in 530BC but destroyed during the early Byzantine era (► 17). From its platform, you can take in the wonderful coastal panorama, over-looking the Bay of Edremit and the Greek island of Lésvos.

The majority of the city's remains lie below the temple. You'll need to travel out of Assos village, following signs for Behramkale, to reach them. The city walls and necropolis will come into view on your left, in front of a plateau containing several remains dating from the 4th century BC. Further down towards sea level is a renovated Roman theatre.

At the foot of the cliff, nestled against its very rock, is the port of Behramkale. It used to be a sleepy fishing harbour with just a few 18th-century stone houses, but in the 1980s Istanbul intellectuals made it their weekend hideaway and it was forced to modernise. It's certainly worth having a drink at the waterside even if you don't stay the night in this expensive, but romantic, place.

➕ 180 A2 ✉ 105km (65 miles) south of Çanakkale ⏰ Summer daily 8:30–7; rest of year 8:30–5:30 🚌 To Assos village from Çanakkale and Edremit 💲 Moderate

🎱 Truva (Troy)

The lure of visiting the once great city described by Homer is one few people can resist, yet despite its fame, many visitors find Troy is rather a disappointment, especially if they've seen the magnificent city shown in the movie *Troy* (2004).

Now little more than an assortment of fragments, the site is most notable for being the birthplace of modern archaeology. Heinrich Schliemann followed geographical clues in Homer's tales, and, in 1871, found the remains of an ancient city that seemed to fit the bill. He then set about proving his theory by digging for evidence, a method that became a standard approach to archaeology.

Troy was rebuilt on the same site many times over, resulting in a confusing mass of remains; only a sturdy stone wall dating from about 1500BC remains in one piece. The other attractions are more modern: a large wooden horse (a reference to the Homeric legend of the storming of Troy, when Greek soldiers entered the besieged town by

hiding in a wooden horse that they had ostensibly presented as a gift). You'll also find a model of Homer's Troy and a plaque showing the several historic phases of the city.

➕ 180 A2 ✉ 30km (19 miles) south of Çanakkale ⏰ May–Oct daily 8:30–7; Nov–Apr 9:30–5 💲 Moderate

🎱 Gelibolu Milliparkı (Gallipoli National Park)

The Gallipoli peninsula, now a national park, witnessed one of the fiercest and most infamous battles in World War I. Visitors come to see the 20 or so war cemeteries and memorials that nestle among its sandy beaches and pine-clad hills. Each is dedicated to soldiers of a specific nationality or regiment who fought in the campaign. Tour groups spend three or four hours at the Australian and New Zealand Army Corps (ANZAC) and impressive Turkish memorials, and then at Anzac Cove where the Allied troops made their ill-fated landings. The British and French memorials lie at the very southern tip of the peninsula, about 25km (15 miles) further south, and are off the organised tour route. If you want to spend more time at Gallipoli it's best to take your car on the frequent ferry across the Dardanelles from Çanakkale and explore the area yourself. The visitor centre at Kabatepe sets the area in context.

➕ 180 A3 ✉ On the southern tip of the Gelibolu (Gallipoli) peninsula ⏰ Visitor centre: Tue–Sun 8:30–5:30; memorials: daily dawn–dusk 🚌 From Çanakkale 🚢 To Kabatepe 💲 Free. Guided tours from Çanakkale: expensive

For Kids
• A trip to **Donkey Island** near Çeşme (► Top tips, page 71)
• A **horse-drawn carriage** ride along the Kordon promenade in İzmir (► 72)
• Playing on the sandy beaches of the **Çeşme peninsula** (► 70–71)

Where to... Stay

Prices

Expect to pay for two people sharing a double room

£ under US$130   ££ US$130–US$230   £££ more than US$230

İZMİR

Balçova Thermal Hotel ££

Located 9km (6 miles) from the teeming centre of İzmir, Balçova is a spa resort. The hotel is built around the hot springs, and offers two huge pools, plus many other keep-fit inducements. Less plush, and more affordable than its neighbour, the Termal Princess Otel, the Balçova Thermal provides rest, relaxation and spa cures for everyone from visiting business-people to families.

➕ 182 B4 ☒ Hüseyin Öğütçen Caddesi, Vali Balçova 35330
☎ 0232 259 0102; fax: 0232 259 0829; www. balcovatermal.com
🕙 All year

Crowne Plaza ££

This luxury high-rise tower hotel is 5km (3m) from the downtown core and offers an excellent range of facilities including pool and a shuttle into town. Rooms are comfortable and modern with excellent views from the full-length windows.

➕ 182 B4 ☒ İnciralti Mevkii 10, Sok Balçova ☎ 0232 292 1300; fax: 0232 292 1313; www.ichotelsgroup.com

AYVALIK

Ortunç £

A private location on a sandy blue-flag beach, and only 22 clean, simple rooms make Ortunç popular with visitors looking for peace and the luxury of clear water in which to frolic. Located in a pine-forest clearing, and run by a house-proud ex-opera singer, Ortunç is not really for kids, being instead a place of contemplation and absolute relaxation.

➕ 180 B1 ☒ Alibey Adasi, Ayvalik
🕙 May–Oct: 0266 327 1120; fax: 0266 327 2082 🕙 May–Oct

BEHRAMKALE

Kervansaray Hotel ££

The tiny harbour at Behramkale (near the ancient site of Assos, ▶ 73–74) is heart-breakingly pretty. Kervansaray, one of five hotels fashioned out of the old stone-built warehouses here, may not be the plushest of the bunch but scores high for its comfortable atmosphere and facilities, which include air-conditioning and an outdoor pool in the summer, and fireplaces and a sauna in the winter. As the (mainly Turkish) guests attest, it's a lovely place to spend a romantic weekend.

➕ 180 A2 ☒ Assos–İskele Mevkii, Behramkale, Ayvacik, Çanakkale
☎ 0286 721 7093; fax: 0286 721 7200; info@assoskervansaray.com
🕙 All year

FOÇA

Hotel Club Phokaia £££

Only 10 minutes by taxi from central Foça, and geared to an international, package-tour, family clientele, Phokaia stands out because of its location, smart, sensitive design and professional staff. Many French guests come to stay and the food is of a comparatively high standard, making eating in the hotel's restaurant an attractive option. The Phokaia has 172 rooms and offers every conceivable facility, including fitness suite, several restaurants, five bars and a children's club.

➕ 182 B5 ☒ 2 Mersinaki Koyu, Foça, İzmir ☎ 0232 812 8080; fax: 0232 812 8090; www.phokaia.com
🕙 All year

Where to...
Eat and Drink

Prices
Expect to pay for a three-course meal, excluding drinks
£ under US$15   ££ US$15–US$25   £££ more than US$25

ÇEŞME

Alaçatı Taş Otel £££

This 100-year-old mansion has been converted with care into a pretty small hotel that's a haven from the busy resort. The stone floors and whitewashed walls are full of character, and homey touches, and the bedrooms are individually styled with beautiful linens and contemporary bathrooms.
There's a shady garden with a good-sized pool.

➕ 182 A4 ✉ Kemalpaşa caddesi 132, Yeni Mecidiye Mahallesi, Alaçatı 35950 ☎ 0232 716 7717; fax: 0232 716 8517; www.tashotel.com
🕓 All year

Sheraton Çeşme Hotel, Resort & Spa £££

The flagship spa hotel in this historic spa centre, the Sheraton offers 3km (2 miles) of majestic beachfront plus a Thermalife spa and thalassotherapy (sea water therapy) centre with massive indoor pool, plus ten restaurants and 24-hour room service. The plush guest rooms are housed in three high-rise wings.

➕ 182 A4 ✉ Sifne Caddesi 35, Ilıca 35940 ☎ 0232 723 1240; fax: 0232 723 1856; www.starwoodhotels.com
🕓 All year

ÇANAKKALE

Kolin Hotel ££

A sparkling new large hotel overlooking the water, Kolin offers comfortable modern styled accommodation with a large open-air swimming pool and gardens leading to the sea.
Amenities at the Kolin include four restaurants and three bars. There is a vitamin bar at the on-site gym, and this is where you'll also find a *hamam*, Jacuzzi, a sauna and an indoor pool.

➕ 180 A3 ✉ Kepez, Çanakkale 17100 ☎ 0286 218 0808; fax: 0286 218 0800; www.kolinhotel.com
🕓 All year

İZMIR

Deniz Resoran £££

İzmir's best seafood restaurant, Deniz Resoran is smack on the waterfront and is perfect for special lunches and slap-up suppers. Local fish predominate on the display, often complemented by huge local prawns (*karides*), offered sweetly grilled or boiled with rich butter sauce. Wines are relatively expensive: Doluca Reserve is made locally and partners fish prettily.

➕ 182 B4 ✉ Kordon, Atatürk Caddesi 188-B, İzmir ☎ 0232 422 0601 🕓 Daily 9am–11.30pm

Pizza Venedik £

Families predominate at İzmir's most popular pizza restaurant. Reservations are not taken, but Venedik is big and bustling, and you'll rarely have to wait more than a few minutes for a table. Tables on the street are the perfect place to enjoy a beer and a simple margherita pizza. Alternatively, try the Deniz, the house speciality – this pizza comes topped with delicious local clams, prawns and squid.

➕ 182 B4 ✉ 1382 Gül Sokak 10-B, Alsancak, İzmir ☎ 0232 422 2735 🕓 Daily 9.30am–11pm

FOÇA

Celep Restaurant £

Of all the harbourfront restaurants and cafés in Foça, Celep provides the best affordable snacks and meals, the friendliest service and best vantage-point for watching the spectacularly pretty sunsets – although nearby Milano, see below, is a close competitor. Celep is a *mezze*-and-grills place, and is known for its fish, though you can linger over a drink and a snack if you wish.

➕ 182 B5 ✉ Küçükdeniz Sahil Caddesi 50, Foça ☎ 0232 812 1495 🕙 May–Sep daily 11am–1am; 11–11, rest of year. Closed in the daytime if Ramadan is during winter months

Pizza Milano £

If you want a change from traditional Turkish food, Milano offers good Italian-style pizza, with top marks for the seafood-laden Marinara. The establishment is perfectly happy for you to while away the day over coffee, drinks and snacks during quiet (non-mealtime) periods.

➕ 182 B5 ✉ Küçükdeniz Sahil Caddesi 58, Foça ☎ 0232 812 2939 🕙 May–Sep daily 11am–1am; 11–11, rest of year. Closed in the daytime if Ramadan is during the winter months

AYVALIK

Lale Restaurant/Bay Nihatler'in ££

Expertly run by Nihat Bey, Lale, on Alibey Adası just offshore from Ayvalık, is an exemplary Turkish fish restaurant on an island famous for them. Fishing snacks tie up alongside Lale's canopied veranda; inside, it's pretty, clean and very chic. From the 40 or so starters on offer, spinach stewed in olive oil and minty *haydari* (a garlic and yoghurt dish) stand out but the extraordinary fish soup, octopus *köfte*, squid stuffed with cheese,

and clams in butter sauce also demand to be tried. Just-caught local fish are offered either simply grilled or fried. Reservations are essential here.

➕ 180 B1 ✉ Alibey Adası, Ayvalık ☎ 0266 327 1063 / 327 1777; fax: 0266 327 1314 🕙 May–1 Oct daily noon–1am; noon–4, 6–midnight, rest of year. Closed during Ramadan

ÇANAKKALE

Yalova Liman Restaurant ££

On the first floor above Çanakkale's small fish market (beside the car ferry exit), Yalova affords views over to Europe at Kilitbahir. You can choose from 35 starters, hot and cold, perhaps *samphire* (sea asparagus) if in season, with minced garlic, or stunning *semisoto* (purslane leaves and yoghurt). The hot starters also show the chef's deft hand. A big fish (agree the price first) or a few fried *barbunya* (red or grey mullet) are

definitely worth tasting, as is the fine wine selection. Try Sarafin, a world-class wine made on the shores opposite.

➕ 180 A3 ✉ Gumruk Sokak 7, Çanakkale ☎ 0286 217 1045; fax: 0286 217 6360 🕙 Daily noon–midnight

ÇEŞME

Yusuf Usta Ev Yemakları ££

This is one of the best places for Turkish food in the area, try the tempting home cooked dishes on display or choose a juicy kebap or simple roast chicken served with fresh salad. The *pide* makes a great snack at any time of the day. There's a shady garden for eating al-fresco during spring and summer and a pretty dining room for rainy low season days.

➕ 182 A4 ✉ Ataturk Caddesi, Zeytinci Is Merkezi 1, Alaçatı ☎ 0232 726 8823 🕙 Daily 11am–11pm

Where to...
Shop

İZMİR

İzmir's bazaar is more authentic and slightly less expensive than that of Istanbul though its mass of narrow alleyways and streets make it more difficult to find your way around. There's less jewellery and more handicrafts, including excellent *kilims*, copperware, brass, ceramics, onyx and wood. **Kızlarağası Han** on Kemeraltı, a former 18th-century coaching inn has hundreds of stalls and shops offering Turkish handicrafts and souvenirs. There is a Turkish Ministry of Culture (**DOSIM**) shop (tel: 0232 484 3692) next to the PTT (post office) on Cumhuriyet Meydanı that stocks high-quality Turkish handicrafts.

ÇEŞME

On the Çeşme peninsula, which grows the only mastic trees in Turkey, you can buy **mastic jam** and **mastic rakı**, neither of which are found anywhere else. The town's main street, **İnkilap Caddesi**, is lined with shops selling these and other Turkish souvenirs.

AYVACIK

Ayvacık (not to be confused with Ayvalık) is the headquarters of the pioneering **DOBAG carpet project** (Cannakale Caddesi, tel: 0286 712 1274, open daily 9–5). DOBAG carpets are of the highest quality and this is reflected in the prices.

BERGAMA

Bergama is renowned for its deep red carpets. These are sold in numerous shops in the old town but prices are more expensive than elsewhere in Turkey – so haggle well.

Where to...
Be Entertained

FESTIVALS, THE ARTS, NIGHTLIFE

İzmir is the focus for cultural activities. The **Atatürk Cultural Centre** is home to a symphony orchestra and the city also hosts the **State Ballet and Opera Company** (tel: 0232 484 3692). The **International İzmir Festival** is held in June. Contact the city tourist office.

Rain Club (1649 Kokak Turan 79, Karşıyaka, İzmir; www.rain-club.com) is the city's leading club with open-air dance floors and several restaurants.

BOAT TRIPS

Tickets for trips to the Greek islands of **Lesvos** and **Chios** are sold at travel agencies on the harbourfronts of Ayvalık and Çeşme respectively. You may need to leave your passport with the excursion's organisers the night before you travel (➤ panel, page 73). You can also take rides along the coast at Foça; buy tickets from the boat's captain in the harbour.

WATER SPORTS

Scuba-diving is established at **Ayvalık**, where the Ayvalık Palas Hotel (tel: 0266 312 1064) hires out equipment and offers instruction, and at **Çeşme**, where Aquarius Dive Centre has an office close to the seafront (Yalı Caddesi, tel: 0232 712 1050). Ayvalık's breezy peninsula also attracts **windsurfers**, especially to Alaçatı, 11km (7 miles) south of the town.

South Aegean

Getting Your Bearings

Characterised by rocky, pine-clad peninsulas and calm river deltas, the Southern Aegean also offers good beaches and clear seas. The footprints of history can be seen at every turn, and the region has perhaps the greatest concentration of ancient attractions outside Istanbul. This is Turkey's oldest and most popular tourist region, with a well-established tourist infrastructure to draw the crowds.

If you want a hedonistic resort with neon-lit bars, or a sunbed among thousands of others to soak in the sun, then you'll find it here. Sadly, the rush to accommodate this sudden influx of foreign visitors has resulted in some ugly modern development that has marred parts of the coastline.

However, the region hasn't been spoiled yet.

**Previous page:
The "furious
Medusa" at the
Temple of
Apollo, Didim
(Didyma)**

**Left: The once-
magnificent
Temple of
Apollo at Didim**

Historical attractions include Ephesus, the biggest crowd-puller in Turkey, whose temple was one of the wonders of the world. The fountains at Pamukkale and the nearby ancient site of Aphrodisias make a great day trip from the coast and as you travel around you'll see swathes of sunflowers and cotton growing on the wide coastal plains.

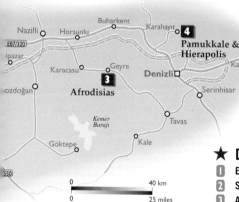

Above: The Temple of Serapis at Efes (Ephesus)

Below: The clear waters off Bodrum make the resort popular with divers

You'll be able to enjoy yourself on the water too. There are ample opportunities for diving and other water sports and there's a thriving market in day cruises on a traditional *gület* (schooner). In addition, the resort of Bodrum with its impressive crusader castle makes the perfect starting point for the famed Blue Cruise along the coast.

★ Don't Miss

At Your Leisure

Base yourself at the lively resort of Kuşadası or in Selçuk (further inland with a quieter night scene) for the first two nights to allow ample time to visit Ephesus and the ancient sites in the delta of the River Menderes. On the third day, travel inland to tour Aphrodisias and Pamukkale, staying the night here before moving on to Bodrum.

The South Aegean in Five Days

Day 1

Morning
Rise early and get to the ruins of ❶ Efes (Ephesus, ➤ 84–87) by about 9am. Explore its ancient buildings (right) before the tour buses arrive (usually around 9.30). Allow three to fours hours here, then make your way to Selçuk for lunch at Seçkin (Çengiz Topal Caddesi 26), which has a good reputation for Moroccan food and has a roof terrace.

Afternoon
As the best finds from Ephesus are now on display at the archaeological museum at the nearby town of ❷ Selçuk (➤ 88–89), a visit here is a must. Allow 90 minutes for looking around, then stroll to the Basilica of St John, where the body of the Christian apostle is said to rest. Finally, take a taxi to Meryemana, 7km (4 miles) out of town, reputedly the final home of the Virgin Mary.

Evening
Drive to ❻ Kuşadası (➤ 97) for a tour of its stylish carpet shops or the touristy bazaar. Enjoy a meal of fresh seafood at a waterfront restaurant before heading to Bar Street for drinks and dancing.

Day 2

Morning
Travel south from Kuşadası on the 515 and then the 525 to explore the delta of the River Menderes. Among fields of sunflowers, olives and cotton are three ancient sites: ❽ Priene (➤ 98) in a majestic elevated setting; ❾ Milet (Miletos, ➤ 99–100), with the remains of the largest ancient

theatre in Turkey; and the Temple of Apollo at **10 Didim** (Didyma,
► 100–101), seat of an ancient oracle.

Afternoon
After your tour, head 3km (2 miles) south from
Didyma to the coast. Stop at the resort of
Altınkum for a cool drink and perhaps a swim.

Evening
Return to Kuşadası, and go to the *hamam*
(► 21) for a refreshing massage.

Day 3

Morning
Travel 160km (100 miles) inland on the E87/320 to
Nazilli. Turn right, following signs to the ancient city of
3 Afrodisias (Aphrodisias, ► 90–91). One of the most important schools
of sculpture in the Roman Empire was located here and many impressive
buildings and fine carving (above right) and statuary have been unearthed.

Afternoon
From Afrodisias head south to Tavas, then turn left on to the 330. At
the junction with the E87, turn left, heading for Denizli. From here it's
19km (12 miles) to **4 Pamukkale** (► 92–93). Walk at the top of the
white limestone cascade, swim in one of the mineral pools, have a spa
treatment or explore the mainly Roman remains of Hierapolis.

Day 4

Morning
Head south from Pamukkale towards Bodrum. If it's
Tuesday, stop off at the town of Milas, where a lively
market will be in full swing.

Afternoon
Explore **5 Bodrum** (right, ► 94–96), one of the most
popular and cosmopolitan Turkish resorts. Don't miss
the impressive Petronium, a 15th-century castle, which
houses the Museum of Underwater Archaeology.

Evening
Shop in the chic boutiques then stroll along Meyhaneler
Sokak (Street of Taverns) for live music and good food.

Day 5

Morning/Afternoon
Take a boat out to the Gulf of Gökova to enjoy the clear
waters and secluded bays. After dark, use up any excess
energy at the excellent Disco Halikarnas (► 106).

❶ Efes (Ephesus)

Walk through the preserved streets and explore the opulent
houses of Ephesus, the largest and most complete ancient city
in the eastern Mediterranean. It's also the most visited attraction in Turkey, but don't let this put you off: your fellow
travellers will help to re-create the atmosphere of the once-
bustling city. The compact site cascades down a hillside,
which affords wide-ranging views across the countryside.

**The frieze on
the Temple of
Hadrian depicts
Tyche, the
goddess of
fortune**

Founded in the 11th century BC, Ephesus became renowned
as a place of pilgrimage to Artemis, the goddess of fertility. In
Roman times the city was capital of Asia Minor, a trade and
banking centre, with a population of more than 250,000
people. Almost all the excavated buildings date from this time
(1st to 5th centuries AD). Ephesus remained vibrant until the
6th century, when its port on the River Cayster finally silted,
cutting off the seaways that had been its lifeblood.

Going Downtown

Touring Ephesus is a little like visiting a modern city; its main
streets are named and easy to follow. There are two entrances
but most tour groups start from the top of the hill and, if you
take a taxi from Selçuk, your driver is likely to drop you here.
This allows you to walk down through the remains rather
than climbing uphill – a sensible option, given the heat.

Once beyond the top ticket office, you'll find yourself on a
plateau and in the least interesting part of the site. Don't
despair: follow the path between the barely recognisable

Crowds stroll down Curetes Street, the site's main thoroughfare, to the Library of Celsus

upper *agora* (marketplace) and a colonnaded marble street to reach **Domitian Square,** guarded at its far end by the **Gate of Hercules.** It is from this point that Ephesus changes from just another archaeological site into a discernible city.

A Sophisticated City

Winding down the hill before you is well-preserved **Curetes Street,** the Oxford Street or Fifth Avenue of its day, lined with two long colonnades of

Temple of Artemis

The Temple of Artemis was in many ways the *raison d'être* of Ephesus. A colossal, ornate edifice dedicated to the goddess of fertility, it was one of the seven wonders of the world, said to have measured 105m (345 feet) by 55m (180 feet), with 15m (50-foot) columns. Sadly, little grandeur survives. Goths destroyed it in AD262 and in the 6th century the Byzantine emperor Justinian took most of the marble for his church of Aya Sofya in Istanbul (➤ 42–43).

shops that are interspersed with shrines. Look for the **Temple of Hadrian** on the right, with its distinctive Corinthian columns supporting a vivid frieze of the fortune goddess, Tyche. Narrow alleys lead off towards residential areas, where the houses of rich Ephesians were built on a gradient to take advantage of the cool breezes from the sea. Archaeologists have been renovating tracts of the residential area and **Terraced Houses** feature more than a dozen rooms decorated with exquisite mosaic floors and frescoed walls, all protected by an incongruous modern plastic roof.

The theatre, where St Paul once preached, is now the venue for performances during the Ephesus Festival of Culture and Art

Curetes Street ends in a small, paved square, which forms a focal point for tour groups. This is a great place for photographs because the impressive **Library of Celsus** dominates the skyline. Erected in AD117 as a memorial to Gaius Julius Celsus, a high-ranking Roman, its grandiose two-storey façade, decorated with columns and with statues standing in its alcoves, is still beautiful. Linking the library and the *agora,* the **Gate of Mazeus and Mithridates** – built in the style of a triumphal arch, and topped by a richly ornate frieze – was commissioned by two former slaves as thanks for being made free men by Emperor Augustus. On the opposite side of the square and at the very heart of the city lie buildings whose purpose were a world away from the reverential and monumental – the **Baths of Scholastica** and a brothel, which is indicated by a footprint and a woman's face etched in the pavement near by.

Marble Way, its surface scarred by the passage of ancient cartwheels, runs from the square, past the *agora* to the

theatre. Capable of seating 24,000 people, it has been renovated in modern times – some say overly so – and is the venue for the Ephesus Festival of Culture and Art each May. It's also about the only place where you can sit and rest your feet. Forming an intersection with Marble Way at the theatre is the **Arcadian Way,** which links the town with the harbour 500m (550 yards) away. Street lighting was installed along its route in the 5th century (when only Rome and Antioch had this distinction) but now much of its length, and the old warehouse district beyond, are off-limits to tourists so you'll have to follow a narrow, dusty path left to exit at the lower gate.

Born in a Blaze of Glory

The location of Ephesus was no accident. Its founder Androclus consulted the Oracle at Delphi in Greece before his journey. The enigmatic prediction was that the site of the new city would be indicated "by a fish; follow the wild boar". Exploring near the River Cayster, Androclus and his companions came across some local men barbecuing fish. As they passed, an ember leapt from the fire, which ignited nearby scrubland and spooked a wild boar. Androclus knew he had found his spot!

TAKING A BREAK

Escape the crowds and head to Selçuk for the modest **Park Restoran** in a pretty town-centre park. The simple grills and an idyllic location make it a lovely place to unwind.

🔲 182 B4
✉ 19km (12 miles) northeast of Kuşadası, 3km (2 miles) west of Selçuk
🕐 Daily 8:30–5:30
🍴 Cafés (£) outside both ticket offices; drinks stands within the site
🚌 From Kuşadası and Selçuk drop off at the Tusan Hotel on the main road. There's a 1km (0.5 mile) walk or carriage ride to the lower ticket office
💷 Expensive; Terraced Houses: expensive

Temple of Artemis
✉ 500m (550 yards) from Selçuk on the Kuşadası road
🕐 Daily 8–5
💷 Inexpensive

EFES: INSIDE INFO

Top tips Take water and a hat, as **there is very little shade** from the intense summer heat.
• If you take a taxi to Ephesus, your driver will probably offer you a fare package that also takes in **Meryemana** (➤ 89)

Hidden gem Climb **Bulbul Dağ** (Nightingale Hill), above the ruins to find an ancient city wall, all that is left of the town from the rule of Lysimachus, one of Alexander the Great's generals. Dating from Hellenistic times, it still features impressive gates and towers.

One to miss There's not much left of the **Temple of Artemis** so gaze at it from the site entrance rather than buying an extra ticket to go inside.

2 Selçuk

The little town of Selçuk thrives on its connection with Ephesus (► 84–87) and its excellent Ephesus Museum is the place to really understand more about daily life in the ancient city. Selçuk is also worth visiting for its two important sites with close links to the early development of Christianity.

Ephesus Museum

A statue of the goddess Artemis at the Ephesus Museum in Selçuk

The **museum** is well designed and laid out. Its first room displays a wide range of domestic finds and includes a re-creation of a Roman room excavated at the site – Slope House at Ephesus (► 86) would have been furnished in much the same way.

However, it is the **communal statuary** in the other galleries that really captures the imagination: Room 7 displays statues of the goddess Artemis in her multi-breasted, wide-hipped personification of fertility, while the Hall of the Emperors dramatically rounds off the museum with its ornate decorative frieze, taken from the Parthian Monument, once a neighbour of the Library of Celsus (► 86) in the heart of Ephesus.

Basilica of St John

The ruins of the **Basilica of St John** are only a short walk up the hill behind the museum. It was built in the 6th century within the protective wall of an older citadel to glorify the burial site of the apostle St John the Evangelist. The huge cathedral once rivalled Istanbul's Aya Sofya (► 42–43) in its grandeur. From the ticket office make your way left past the useful information tableau to the remains of the colonnaded atrium (entryway), then walk into the nave. Here, the two-tier marble and brick colonnade gives the best indication of the vast dimensions of the church. Sadly, the magnificent fortress that tops the citadel is now closed to the public.

Meryemana

Lying 7km (4 miles) outside Selçuk, **Meryemana** (House of the Virgin Mary) is an important shrine for Christians and Muslims. Since its discovery in 1891, the tiny Byzantine church has been revered as the last home of the Virgin, drawing pilgrims to kiss its sacred icon. In 1967 Pope Paul VI confirmed its authenticity, and it's recognised by Greek and Russian Orthodox churches. The church, used for Sunday services, is always crowded, so a sense of tranquillity may be lacking, though the surrounding gardens, with a freshwater spring, provide cooling shade.

Visions of the Past

Meryemana may have been lost to history had it not been for a 19th-century German nun called Anna Katharina Emmerich. Already known for her visions, she claimed to have been visited by the Virgin Mary, who revealed to her an image, though not the location, of her final home. Some 50 years later, investigators discovered this tiny chapel on a pine-clad hillside that matched the one in the nun's vision. The foundations proved to date from the 1st century AD.

TAKING A BREAK

Karameşe Restaurant is located opposite the Ali Bey Camii (Mosque) and offers a warm welcome. This is the place for *gözleme* – hot, thin, stretchy, buttery bread, served with various fillings. Cheap, delicious, satisfying and fun!

The ruins of the 6th-century Basilica of St John

Tourist Office
Atatürk Mah, Agora Çarşısı No 35 ☎ 0232 892 6945

Ephesus Museum
🟦 182 B4 ✉ Agora Carsısı
🕐 May–Oct Tue–Sun 8–noon 1–7; Nov–Apr 8–noon, 1–5:30 ☕ Café (£) within the museum 💰 Moderate

Basilica of St John
🟦 182 B4 ✉ St John Sokak
🕐 May–Oct daily 8–7; Nov–Apr 8–5:30 💰 Moderate

Meryemana
🟦 182 B3 ✉ Off route E87, 7km (4 miles) south of Ephesus 🕐 Daily dawn–dusk ☕ Café (£) on site 💰 Free; compulsory parking fee: moderate

Çamlık Open-Air Rail Museum
🟦 182 B3 ✉ Çamlık, Selçuk
🕐 Daily 8:30–6:30 ☎ 0232 894 8116; fax: 0232 894 8021 💰 Inexpensive

---

SELÇUK: INSIDE INFO

Top tip If you are not a pilgrim, **avoid Meryemana's busiest time**, the Feast of the Assumption on 15 August, and Sunday mornings when Mass is held.

In more depth The attractions in this area aren't just archaeological. For something a little different, the **Çamlık Buharlı Lokomotif Müzesi (Çamlık Open-Air Rail Museum)**, 12km (7.5 miles) south of Selçuk, has a collection of about 25 mainly pre-World War II steam engines. Though none are actually in use, you are free to climb aboard many of them for a closer look at the old technology.

3 Afrodisias

(Aphrodisias)

The sophisticated city of Aphrodisias was renowned throughout the Hellenistic and Roman empires for its school of sculpture and art. Comparatively recent excavation work means that most of its treasures are still intact, and a prodigious amount of monumental statuary can still be admired in the on-site museum.

Aphrodisias sprang up in the 7th century BC around the cult of Aphrodite, goddess of love and fertility. A seam of especially fine marble nearby helped the school to meet demand for decorative statuary throughout the Mediterranean – works attributed to it have been found as far west as Spain. Begun by the Greeks, the city caught the eye of the Romans, who adapted many of the buildings to their own style. But despite its wealth and cultural importance, the city was vulnerable to attacks and earthquakes. The city foundered during the 1st millennium AD after several earthquakes, and the Mongul ruler Tamerlane sounded its final death knell in 1402.

Make your way left out of the museum square to the **theatre,** a white marble semicircle built into the slope of a natural hill. The *cavea* (seating area) and stage, both Roman additions, hidden for centuries under 40m (130 feet) of soil, are well preserved. The path leads on past the **South Agora,** an

Left: The stadium at Afrodisias is the best preserved in Turkey

Something for Everyone

The word "stadium" comes from a measurement of about 200m (220 yards), the length of the shortest running race in ancient Greece. After a while, the word was used to describe the arena in which competitions took place. Aphrodisias stadium was designed to showcase popular Greek sports such as wrestling, boxing and athletics, but it was also the scene of Roman chariot racing and gladiatorial combat. After the town theatre was damaged by the 7th-century earthquake, the stadium was used for circuses and shows.

open square whose limits are defined by the **Tiberius Portico**, a magnificent colonnade erected in the 1st century AD. A left turn at the southwestern corner leads north, past **Hadrian's Baths** (still with their floor tiles) and through a jumble of colossal building blocks strewn across the path. **The Temple of Aphrodite** lies ahead on the right. It's still standing, but this major sanctuary to the "protectress" of the city – later converted into a Byzantine basilica by the addition of an altar – is off-limits to the public.

The impressive **stadium** is the northern-most point of your visit. At more than 260m (280 yards) long and 60m (66 yards) wide, it is larger than any classical stadium in Turkey (► panel, page 90). Its stands, capable of seating more than 30,000 spectators, are exceptionally well preserved.

The crowning glory of the site is the **tetrapylon,** a monumental double archway built in the 2nd century AD at an important road intersection and re-erected in 1990. The 16 fluted supporting columns are carved with exceptional skill and the pediments still display their original detail.

Aphrodisias' **museum** is well worth its extra entry fee. Displaying some of the city's finest statuary, it exhibits works by the masters and apprentice pieces by their pupils. As the school produced monumental statuary for temples and public spaces, it's no surprise to find a plethora of gods and politicians here.

Left: Detail of a sarcophagus

Below: The elegant 2nd-century AD tetrapylon is one of the site's treasures

TAKING A BREAK

If you want to cool down with a drink, there's a shady **café opposite the museum.** For something more substantial, the French-run **Aphrodisias Hotel** (► 102–103) on the Karacasu road serves simple, tasty food.

🔢 183 D3 ⊠ 140km (87 miles) east of Kuşadası via the E87/320 and R585 🕐 May–Oct daily 8:30–7; Nov–Apr 8:30–5 💰 Aphrodisias: moderate; museum: moderate

---

AFRODISIAS: INSIDE INFO

Top tip A clockwise tour is signposted around the site, which, including the museum, should take around 3 hours.

Hidden gem Near the *tetrapylon* is **the tomb of Dr Kenan Tevfik Erim**, the Turkish archaeologist who made Aphrodisias his life's work. He was invited to document the site in 1961 and stayed for nearly 30 years, organising the numerous excavations that brought the beautiful ancient city to light. When he died in 1990, his dedication was rewarded with a resting place at the heart of his beloved city.

4 Pamukkale and Hierapolis

Nature has worked its magic in the foothills of the River Menderes. A huge waterfall tumbles over reflective limestone, which is the colour of newly fallen snow. Visible from far across the surrounding countryside, its stalactites and shallow pools shimmer in the sunlight, their fringes shining like a cut diamond. The Turks named this rare geological feature Pamukkale, which means "cotton castle" because of its resemblance to a fluffy mass of their prime autumn crop.

Pamukkale is fed by a mineral-rich freshwater spring emanating from a higher plateau. As the water cascades down the valley it deposits a mineral film on the rocks, which, over millions of years, developed into a seam of limestone several metres thick, creating a travertine waterfall. Though its location was known since antiquity, it was the Romans who first exploited the waters, building a thermal spa around the spring. This settlement rapidly became the city of Hierapolis.

Pamukkale
The advent of tourism in the 1970s put Pamukkale on the map. Visitors would clamber around at will, damaging the limestone and leaving deposits of sun oil in the freshwater pools. A rash of modern hotels at the top of the falls diverted the springs to feed their swimming pools and the water reaching the cascade diminished in quantity and quality. By the early 1990s, it was losing its brilliance and its outer fringes were becoming overgrown with lichen.

Serious and sustained intervention by the Turkish authorities is now reviving the cascade. Unesco has not put the site on it's list of endangered monuments; happy with the management plan that's been put into place. The hotels have been bulldozed and the waters redirected to feed the damaged sections and gradually restore their lustre. Visitors can walk only on one narrow pathway through the pools, without shoes – an uncomfortable experience for most. But despite the damage, it's still a remarkable and beautiful phenomenon – nothing can match the play of light across its surfaces.

Above: Limestone deposits from mineral-rich waters have created the spectacular travertine waterfall at Pamukkale

Left: Relax among the genuine Roman columns at the modern thermal pool in Hierapolis

Hierapolis

The remains of the Roman city of Hierapolis (which means "holy city") are scattered along the top of the Pamukkale plateau. There is a fine 2nd-century theatre on the western hillside. A necropolis of more than 1,200 scattered tombs lies to the northwest, one of the largest contemporary burial sites in Asia Minor. The small museum on the site (Tue–Sun 8–noon, 12:30–6) displays a range of finds from the area.

TAKING A BREAK

The tastiest food in Pamukkale is served at the **Weisse Burg** (➤ 104). There are plenty of vegetarian options, and even a few rooms for the night.

🚩 183 E4

✉ 220km (137 miles) east of Kuşadası

🕐 24 hours; ticket office manned daily 8–7 (5 Nov–Apr) 🚌 From Denizli to bottom of cascade

🍴 Café (£) at the thermal baths 🎟 Combined ticket to cascade and Hierapolis: moderate

Pamukkale Thermal Baths

🕐 May–Oct daily 9–7; 9–5 rest of year 🎟 Moderate

PAMUKKALE AND HIERAPOLIS: INSIDE INFO

Top tips The best place to view the pools is from above so **don't park at the bottom of the falls**. Drive on past the village, turn right at the South Gate reception centre for the North Gate, 500m (550 yards) beyond. From here, it's 1,500m (1,640 yards) to the parking area for the upper cascade and Hierapolis.
• Don't go near the falls after dark as there are some steep, unfenced drops.

In more depth Take to the waters at **Pamukkale Thermal Baths** on the plateau, a modern complex on the site of the sacred spring. For a small fee, you can swim among the fallen and submerged columns of the original Roman spa.

⑤ **Bodrum**

Bodrum, despite vast tourist development of it's surrounding peninsula, remains one of the prettiest resorts in Turkey. The old part of town, with its whitewashed stone buildings draped in bright bougainvillaea and fragrant honeysuckle, retains a bohemian atmosphere, while the yachting fraternity love the myriad rocky coves and sandy beaches nearby. Still popular with wealthy Turks who spend the summer at their villas, it's been called Turkey's St Tropez.

Package tourists have flocked here since the 1980s and the town, resisting the pressure to build high, has spread out to incorporate several villages in nearby bays. This "greater Bodrum" is now one of the largest holiday resorts in the Eastern Mediterranean and in high season satellite resorts such as Bitez and Gümbet are a magnet for young Brits, devoted to the hedonistic pleasures of bronzing and boozing. For a Turkish atmosphere, stay in the old town.

An Ancient Wonder
On the site of modern Bodrum stood ancient Halicarnassus, founded in the

11th-century BC. It later became renowned as the location of one of the seven wonders of the world: the majestic funerary monument of its ruler Mausolus (*c*376–353), which gives us the word "mausoleum". Most people who venture to the site of the **mausoleum** today are disappointed by what remains, as much of the stone was taken to construct the vast, medieval castle on the isthmus in the harbour. This splendid fortification, called the **Petronium** (from which the name "Bodrum" is derived), is now much more interesting than the more-famous mausoleum. It was built by the "crusading" Knights Hospitallers of St John (► panel, page 120) who made this part of Turkey home in the early 15th century. Today, it hosts the fascinating **Museum of Underwater Archaeology,** the largest of its kind in the world. Several medieval chambers display finds from wrecks dating from the Mycenaean and Bronze Ages through to the Byzantine era. All were discovered in the waters around Turkey. You can also visit rooms containing salvaged artefacts and, if you dare, enter the dungeons.

Below left: Relaxing on a traditional *gület* in Bodrum harbour

Below: Bodrum's castle, built by the Knights Hospitallers of St John in the 15th century

A Modern Wonder
Bodrum's busy marina is vibrant at all times of day but it really comes alive around sunset and into the early hours. In the narrow streets of the old town around **Meyhaneler Sokak** (Street of the Taverns), you'll find chic boutiques and souvenir shops along with rustic restaurants. If the fancy takes you, join the crowd later and take in a nightclub. **Disco Halikarnas** on Cumhuriyet Caddesi is the best in the eastern Mediterranean and shouldn't be missed.

The Blue Cruise
It's exciting to explore the Turkish coast by boat. You can spend a few days sailing into small harbours for lunch, into empty bays for an afternoon swim, and enjoy a romantic

Where History Began
Bodrum was the home town of Herodotus (485–425BC), "the father of history". He travelled extensively throughout Asia Minor, Babylonia, Egypt and Greece, making copious notes about their buildings, legends, past events and traditions, which he organised into a vast tome entitled *History* (meaning "enquiry" in Greek).

Bodrum is a popular base for boat trips and its marina is always busy with touring yachts

dinner on board in the evening. It's a popular pastime for Turks too because of a book by Bodrum native Cevat Şakir Kabaağaçlı called *Mavi Yolculuk* (The Blue Cruise or Voyage). Written in the 1920s, it charts life on the waters around the Aegean and Turquoise coasts.

Today a water-based holiday is as easy to arrange as a land-based stay either by pre-booking a boat or hiring one when you arrive. If you have a day skipper's certificate you can rent a bare boat (without crew), but prices are surprisingly reasonable for a crewed *gület* (traditional Turkish schooner) and this takes the hard work out of getting around; they'll even cater so you don't have to lift a finger. Try S&J Travel, Neyzen Tefvik Caddesi 218 (tel: 0252 316 0561), who are specialists in custom *gület* trips.

TAKING A BREAK

Sakallı Köfteci, on Yeni Çarşi (just off busy Kale Cadessi) is a Bodrum institution. Join the locals for *köfte* and soup between 11am and 6pm.

➕ 182 B2

Tourist Office
✉ Bariş Meydani No 48, near the castle
☎ 0252 316 1091

Petronium
✉ On the harbourfront 🕒 Tue–Sun 8:30–noon, 1–5:30
🍴 Two cafés (£) inside 💷 Moderate. Museum: moderate

Mausoleum
✉ Signposted from Neyzen Tefvik Caddesi shore road on the west flank of the harbour
🕒 Tue–Sun 8:30–noon 1–5 💷 Inexpensive

Disco Halikarnas
✉ Intersection Cumhuriyet Caddesi and Zeki Müren Sokak
🕒 Daily 9pm–late
💷 Expensive

BODRUM: INSIDE INFO

Top tips There's a **one-way traffic system** through town, so it's much easier to leave the car at your hotel and walk.

• Some museum halls at the Petronium are closed at weekends so **visit the castle between Tuesday and Friday** if you can.

One to miss The site of **the mausoleum** is a disappointment – skip it to spend more time soaking in the atmosphere around the harbourfront.

At Your Leisure

Tiny Güvercin Adası (Pigeon Island) is linked to Kuşadası by a causeway

Three Places to Escape the Crowds
• Bafa Gölü (Lake Bafa, ➤ 159) – where donkeys still outnumber cars
• Dilek peninsula (➤ below) – take to the hills and avoid the beaches
• Out to sea (➤ 106) – cruising on a chartered yacht

6 Kuşadası

Kuşadası has something of a dual personality and is the type of place that you'll either love or hate. It's the Turkish Aegean's major cruise port and one of the largest package holiday resorts in Turkey. The tiny old town, based around an Ottoman *kervansary* (now a hotel), has some terrific stylish shops catering for short-stay cruisers, but there's a sprawl of characterless modern hotels and apartments around the town with a young,

boisterous, mainly foreign, clientele whose holiday is one long party. Having said that, it's a useful base, with good restaurants and hotels, and good transport connections to the region's ancient sites.

In Turkish, Kuşadası means "Bird Island", and the town was originally named after a tiny, fortified rock lying just offshore, now linked to the mainland by a causeway (confusingly, the island is called Güvercin Adası or Pigeon Island). On the island, you'll find a diminutive 14th-century citadel.

🔢 182 B3

Tourist Office
✉ Liman Caddesi No 13, opposite the harbour entrance ☎ 0256 614 1103

Kuşadası Castle
✉ Güvercin Adası (Pigeon Island) in the harbour 🕐 Summer Tue–Sun 9–8; winter 9–5 💷 Inexpensive

7 Dilek Yarımadası/Büyük Menderes Deltası Milliparkı

A long pine-clad finger of land, 25km (16 miles) south of Kuşadası, points west into the Aegean Sea as if remonstrating with the Greek island of Sámos just offshore. Much of the Dilek peninsula has escaped human interference, and 27,000ha (66,700 acres) of its mountain peaks and deep valleys have been designated a national park, preserving populations of rare and endangered animals such as bears, wild horses and Anatolian leopards (*Panthera pardus tulliana*). This has recently been combined with the 9,800ha (24,200 acres) of the Büyük Menderes Deltasi Milliparkı on the flat plains to the south, which protects important environments for endemic and migratory bird species. Much of the far-western section of the park is also a military base and off-limits to the public, however, so if you hope to spot one of these elusive creatures, you'll probably be disappointed.

The cycling opportunities are excellent (but there are no facilities here to rent bicycles, so you'll have to hire yours in Kuşadası), as is the hiking on marked trails, especially in the central Sarıkaya Canyon.

🏛 182 B3 ✉ 28km (17 miles) south of Kuşadası 🕐 Jun–Sep daily 8:30–7; Oct–May 8:30–5. No overnight camping 🍴 Beach bars on the peninsula (£), or cafés at Güzelçamlı (£) outside the national park 🚌 *Dolmuş* from Kuşadası every 15 or 30 minutes, 8–6 in summer 💰 Inexpensive

8 Priene

If the busy streets of Ephesus make you yearn for solitude and shade, then Priene is the perfect antidote. The remains of this delightful 2,500-year-old city, overlooking delta of the River Menderes, benefit from fresh sea breezes and nestle among hundreds of fragrant pine trees

Segments of columns lie scattered around the Temple of Athena at Priene

For Kids
• Making a splash at **Adaland Waterpark and Dolphin Park** in Kuşadası (► 106)
• Exploring the ramparts of the **Petronium** in **Bodrum** (► 95)
• Take a coastal **boat trip** (► 106)

huddled beneath rocky peaks. Most importantly, perhaps, Priene is not yet on the itinerary of large tour groups.

In the 4th century BC, when the original coastal port became land-locked, a new and higher city was built. It was laid out in a grid pattern that was based on the new theories of town planning pioneered by Hippodamus of Miletos (► panel, page 99) and, unlike other

Best Beaches
• Kadınlar Plajı (Ladies' Beach), 3km (2 miles) from Kuşadası
• Gümbet, near Bodrum, with its young, predominantly British, clientele
• Altınkum, 3km (2 miles) south of Didyma, for family fun

(marketplace) and up to a tiny, well-preserved theatre. The tumbledown walls of family homes hug the hillside beyond; Alexander's lodging lies in the lower western section.

Don't forget to take a walk above the main town to the ruined Temple of Demeter. From here the views across the valley are spectacular.

🚩 182 B3 ✉ 37km (23 miles) south of Kuşadası on route 09-55 🕐 May–Oct daily 8:30–6; Nov–Apr 8:30–5 🍴 Café 200m (220 yards) from ticket office 🚌 From Söke 🎫 Inexpensive

🟨 Milet (Miletos)

During the Greek era, Miletos was the principal port of entry into Asia Minor and far outweighed Ephesus in influence, but the city was suffocated by mud from the River Menderes, rendering its buildings landlocked. The theatre at Miletos is one of the finest built during the Roman era but, aside from this *tour de force*, this isn't the place to come if you like ancient sites to be breathtaking and dramatic.

It's the overall dimensions of the theatre that are most impressive. The front wall was originally 140m (153 yards) long and would have concealed the interior stage and

The magnificent theatre illustrates the importance of ancient Milet (Miletos)

ancient cities, was not modified by the Romans.

An early visitor was Alexander the Great, who used it as his base for a consultation with the great oracle at nearby Didyma (▶ 100). Alexander was obviously impressed, because he donated money for the construction of the Temple of Athena, now the most important monument at Priene. Several columns have been re-erected and it can be reached along the central street, which is connected to a well-worn path uphill from the ticket office. A series of straight thoroughfares and alleyways around the temple cover the plateau site and lead down to the *stoa* (a roof supported by columns), and city *agora*

The Best Laid Plans

Hippodamus of Miletos, who lived in the 5th century BC, was the first architect to design settlements on a grid system. His proposals for straight and intersecting streets made urban living easier and his ideas became a model for town planning, influencing numerous ancient Greek cities as well as, more recently, the boulevards of Paris and avenues of New York.

orchestra, but much of the central section has collapsed. What's left of the *cavea* (seating area) is still supported by huge vaulted passageways (*parados*), through which audiences arrived and left. These are intact, runing in a semicircle behind the seating, and open at both ends so that you can explore the interior.

The easiest way to understand the layout of the city is by walking across the flat land behind the theatre to take a look at the site from the former harbour, though the route can be muddy in spring. Along the barely discernible Sacred Way, which linked Miletos with Didyma (▶ right), you can explore the *agora*, gymnasium and partially re-constructed Ionic *stoa*. Alternatively, drive to the ticket office and café

area for a great view of the theatre without entering the site at all.

➕ 182 B3 ✉ Route 09-55, 40km (25 miles) south of Kuşadası 🕐 May–Oct daily 8:30–6, Sep–Apr 8:30–5. Museum closes 30mins before rest of site 🍴 Cafés (£) by the ticket office 🚌 From Söke 🎫 Moderate

🔟 Didim (Didyma)

Perhaps the most impressive single monument on the west coast, the Temple of Apollo at Didyma was home to a powerful oracle whose influence spread throughout the ancient Greek world. When the temple was destroyed by the Persians in 494BC, its Fountain of Prophesy

The grand portico of the Temple of Apollo at Didim (Didyma)

ceased to flow until the day Alexander the Great called in for a consultation 40 years later. As soon as he arrived, it was miraculously restored to working order, indicating his divinity, and the oracle proclaimed him the son of Zeus.

Today, the temple seems small, hemmed in by the modern village and surrounded by carpet shops, but once inside, the sheer architectural beauty of the edifice is clear to see. An exquisite marble head, the "furious Medusa", adorns the steps at the entrance to the site, and it has become an emblem of the sôuthern Aegean. A profusion of fine marble columns grace the temple portico. The column pediments are decorated with exceptionally fine carved bas reliefs, along with Greek and Roman inscriptions. From here, two narrow passages lead to a rectangular inner sanctum, an oblong building with carved marble walls, into which only the priests and the oracle were allowed to venture. The whole temple is then surrounded by more than 100 columns. They are still in their original position, though they no longer stand to their full height.

➕ 182 B3 ✉ 57km (35 miles) south of Kuşadası on route 05-99 🕐 May–Oct daily 8:30–6; Sep–Apr 8:30–5 🚌 From Söke 🍴 Cafés (£) outside the site 💷 Moderate

🔟 Diving near Bodrum

The waters around Bodrum are some of the clearest and cleanest in the Mediterranean, offering a relative abundance of sealife, and good visibility for divers. The Turkish authorities are

Off the Beaten Track
The Temple of Zeus is all that can be seen of the Hellenistic city of **Euromos** (open: Tue–Sun 8–5); the rest lies buried under the surrounding hills. It is, however, worth making a slight detour if you are visiting the larger sites at Priene (▶ 98), Miletos (▶ 99) or Didyma (▶ 100). The temple's location among shady olive groves is beautiful and its form is perfect – it was based on the Parthenon in Athens. Best of all, it's as yet undiscovered by tour groups so you may have it all to yourself even though it lies less than 500m (550 yards) from the main Selçuk to Milas road. Look for the single signpost – it's easy to miss. ➕ 182 C3

understandably concerned about underwater archaeological sites being plundered but do allow people to dive at minor ruins with recognised companies. If you have your certification it's just a matter of booking your dives, and for beginners it's a great place to start.

All the diving centres are affiliated to one of the major certifying bodies; PADI (Professional Association of Diving Instructors) is the most common. The basic qualification, the Open Water certificate, takes five days to complete and enables you to dive accompanied by an instructor to depths no greater than 18m (60 feet). Many centres also offer an introductory session commonly known as the "Discover Scuba Programme". This involves half a day of theory and shallow water work, which will give you the chance to try out the basic techniques and see if it's a pastime that you would enjoy.
➕ 182 B2

Diving Aegean Pro-Dive Centre
✉ Neyzen Tevfik Caddesi 174/C, Bodrum ☎ 0252 316 0737; www.aegeanprodive.com

Where to... Stay

Prices
Expect to pay for two people sharing a double room
£ under US$130   ££ US$130–US$230   £££ more than US$230

KUŞADASI

Kismet Hotel £££

With fantastic views over the Aegean coastline, the Kismet sits on a small promontory with landscaped gardens and several private jetties. Once the holiday home of the last Ottoman Sultan, the hotel sets high standards. The rooms and communal areas are plush and luxurious and the restaurant is one of the smartest in the area. Previous guests here have included British royalty and American Presidents.

➕ 182 B4 ☒ Gazi Begendi Balvari 1, Kuşadası 09400 ☎ 0256 618 1290; fax: 0256 618 1295; www.kismet.com.tr
⊙ All year

Muses House Hotel ££

This adult only boutique hotel opened in the village of Kirazli outside Kuşadası in 2006 and adds a touch of sophistication to the accommodation in this buzzing region. Set in an old Greek mansion the hotel has only five rooms, all with contemporary décor, and cosy public rooms for relaxation. The whole property offers history combined with 21st century gadgets like CD players and flat screen TVs. Outside there are two bright courtyard with tables for al-fresco dining, there's also a pool and verdant garden.

➕ 182 B4 ☒ 158 Kirazli Koyu, Kuşadası 09400 ☎ 0256 667 1125; fax: 0256 667 1125; www.museshouse.com ⊙ All year

SELÇUK

Nisanyan Evleri ve Pansiyon £

The village of Şirince (which means "cute") is postcard-pretty and famous for its homemade wines. Two well-known Turkish travel writers have opened their dream hotel here, a gem of a place, filled with antiques and understated creative touches (including hand-made soaps, local-stone showers and frescoed paint effects). The breakfasts are memorable, as is the soaring view. It all adds up to perfect peace and it's very chic too. Choose between the country house-party atmosphere of the hotel or the couple of charming private houses. Note that there are steep steps in the village, making it unsuitable for young children and people who have difficulty walking.

➕ 182 B4 ☒ Şirince, 8km (5 miles) inland from Selçuk ☎ 0232 898 2308; fax: 0232 898 3209; www.nisanyan.com

PAMUKKALE

Colossae Thermal Hotel ££

Colossae Thermal exceeds expectations in the otherwise touristy resort of Karahayit by virtue of its attractive design, professional management and attention to detail. The rooms are unusually large, as is the pool.

➕ 183 E4 ☒ Karahayit, 3km (2 miles) west of the northern entrance to Pamukkale ☎ 0258 271 4156; fax: 0258 271 4250; www.colossaehotel.com ⊙ All year

DIDIM

Medusa House £

This renovated traditional stone house flanks the Temple of Apollo. Rooms are simple but spotlessly clean and there's ample opportunity to relax in the large garden.

➕ 182 B3 ☒ 09270 Didim ☎ 0256 811 0063; fax: 0256 811 0267; www.medusahouse.com ⊙ May–Oct

Where to...
Eat and Drink

BODRUM

Baia Bodrum ££–£££

Set in a satellite village on the Bodrum peninsula, the Baia Bodrum is a large resort hotel set in ample grounds. Rooms have a cool and contemporary feel, and all have a sea view as they are set on a rising ground above the beach. Amenities include a gym, spa and wellness centre, plus for kids there are water slides, a bowling alley and a club in high season (June– September). There are two pools.

➕ 182 B2 ⊠ Gundogan Beldesi, 48400 ☎ 0252 387 9293; fax: 0252 387 7625; www.baiahotels.com 🕐 All year

The Butterfly ££–£££

An intimate modern boutique hotel on a hillside with panoramic Aegean views away from the bustle of the resort centre, The Butterfly makes a perfect retreat for those wanting total relaxation. Rooms are all individually decorated and vary in size but each has a terrace or garden area. There is

an ample pool area with contemporary styling and furnishing.

➕ 182 B2 ⊠ Barcakci, Ulnu Caddesi, 1512 Sokak 24, 48400 ☎ 0252 313 8358; fax: 0252 313 88357; www.butterflybodrum.com 🕐 Mid-Apr to Dec

BAFA GÖLÜ (LAKE BAFA)

Club Natura Oliva ££

This small 30-room hotel is one of the early leading lights of green tourism in Turkey. The styling is all traditional Turkish stone and wood with magnificent lake views from most areas of the property, which has a lake beach for sunbathing and swimming. The rustic rooms are simply furnished, there's a large communal terrace and living room with log fire in winter. The resort produces its own ecological olive oil, which you can buy on site.

➕ 182 B3 ⊠ Kocaorman Mah. 10, Pinarcık Köyü, Milas 48200 ☎ 0252 519 1072; fax: 0252 519 1015; www.clubnatura.com 🕐 All year

little from Kuşadasi's unrelenting town-centre noise.

KUŞADASI

Club Caravanserai Restaurant £££

Set in a 17th-century caravanserai now restored as a hotel, this excellent restaurant serves smart, European meals, enhanced by starched linen and deferential service. The fish is especially good, and comes plain or accompanied by elaborate sauces. Club Caravanserai is also known for its mouth-watering desserts, which sometimes include a delicious dried-fruit compote. The hotel also offers some fine rooms, though they do suffer a

➕ 182 B3 ⊠ Club Caravanserai Hotel, Atatürk Bul. 1, Kuşadasi ☎ 0256 614 4115 🕐 Daily noon–3:30, 6:30–9:30, Apr–Oct

Planet Yucca ££

Fusion food reaches Turkey with Planet Yucca, which combines traditional Turkish hospitality with dishes from Mexico, Italy, China and India – though you'll still find standard Turkish cuisine on the menu. This is a great place for families and groups with diverse tastes to come and eat. There's live music every night late into the evening.

➕ 182 B3 ✉ Saglik Caddesi 65

☎ 0256 612 5730;

www.planetyucca.com

🕐 Daily 8am–1am

Nisanyan Evleri £–££

This delightful country restaurant is a real treat and the views from the terrace across the countryside are your first reward. The limited daily menu concentrates on good quality local ingredients cooked with care. Dishes include tasty lentil soup, slow roasted lamb shank or locally reared chicken. There's also an interesting wine list with a good choice of domestic vineyards. This is only a small establishment, there are only six tables, so booking is essential.

➕ 182 B4 ✉ Şirince, Selçuk (follow signs from the entrance to Şirince)

☎ 0232 898 2308

🕐 Daily 6pm–10pm

Weisse Burg £

The tastiest food in Pamukkale is served in the informal, relaxed rooftop restaurant of this slightly shambolic pansiyon. This is a good place for vegetarians in particular and food lovers in general because it offers authentic food at a bargain price. Go for chef Hacer Hanım's heavenly havuç tarator (yoghurt and carrot salad), her hearty chicken stew, or whatever other creations she's conjured up. Simple rooms are available for the night and there's also a pool.

➕ 183 E4 ✉ Set back from Menderes Caddesi, Pamukkale

☎ 0258 272 2064 🕐 Lunch: Daily noon–2:30. Dinner: Mon–Fri 6:30–10, Sat–Sun 6:30–11

Aphrodisias Hotel ££

If you've chosen to stay near the archaeological site, the Aphrodisias Hotel has something of a monopoly on your custom but fear not: the food served is good. Farmed trout and free-range chicken may be offered, or you could try the excellent lentil and yayla (yoghurt and rice) soups. The kitchen here sticks to what it knows best, so don't expect flashy cooking; instead, enjoy simple dishes, expertly cooked.

➕ 183 E4 ✉ Aphrodisias Hotel, Karacasu Caddesi, Afrodisias

☎ 0256 448 8132; fax: 0256 448 8422

🕐 Daily noon–3, 6:30–9

Denizhan ££–£££

Situated outside of the town on the road to Turgutreis and Yalikavak, Denizhan has earned a reputation for being one of the finest kebap and roast meat restaurants in the region since the late 1990s. The meat is sourced locally from a town called Bandirma – known throughout Turkey for its quality produce.

Denizhan has a characterful dining room for late season and winter meals, or you may prefer the ample terrace which is popular for al-fresco dining during the summer months.

➕ 102 B4 ✉ Konacık, Bodrum

☎ 0252 363 7674; www.denizhan.com

🕐 All year

Gemibaşı Restaurant ££

Instead of patronising the showier, pricier fish restaurants around the harbour, try honest-to-goodness Gemibaşı on Neyzen Tevfik Caddesi. Here, you can sit outside and eat some of the tastiest fish and seafood in town, including big juicy prawns with lemon, parsley and garlic, and tiny octopuses stewed in olive oil. Cooking is spot on, as are the staff. Book in person at lunchtime for an evening table.

➕ 182 B2 ✉ Neyzen Tevfik Caddesi, Bodrum ☎ 0252 316 1220

🕐 May–Sep daily 12:15–11; Oct–Apr Tue–Sun 12:30–3, 7–10:30

Where to...
Shop

KUŞADASI

Kuşadası is the main cruise-ship port for the Turkish coast, and has a lot of large, stylish carpet shops selling large, high-quality silk rugs. You'll find them clustered on the seafront and around the old *kervansary*; one of the best is **Bazaar 54** on Atatürk Caddesi (tel: 0256 612 7259), but be aware that quality doesn't come cheap.

You'll also find **good-quality jewellers** in abundance in Kuşadası, selling both traditional designs and designer names. Many are official stockists of watches like Breitling and Rolex, so you can be sure that what you buy is the genuine article.

The town is also famed for its **leather goods**, notably bags, jackets and trousers. The shops of the small streets leading through the bazaar are crammed with them but make sure you assess the quality of the workmanship, as it varies enormously.

Note that Kuşadası is one of the centres of the **designer copy** market, especially fake watches, jewellery and clothing. More mundane goods, such as designer T-shirts, socks and underwear, are good value and it seems to be *de rigueur* to stock up on these before you return home.

Kuşadası has a traditional **market** every Tuesday and Friday.

Because there are so many British tourists in the area, you can pay for many goods in **pounds sterling**.

SELÇUK

You'll find **carpet stores** opposite the entrance to the Basilica of St John, and many others in Selçuk's maze of back streets. Many shops employ touts to draw in customers

and you'll probably be approached outside the Ephesus Museum (▶ 88–89).

BODRUM

Bodrum is in general a little more **stylish** than Kuşadası, though you can't escape the underwear and T-shirts altogether. The narrow streets of the old town contain boutiques selling traditional clothing and jewellery, and it's fun to browse. You'll also find a number of shops selling 20th-century **collectibles**, such as copper cookware, household implements, small carved window frames (sold as picture frames), which make interesting and unusual souvenirs to take home.

As in Kuşadası, you can pay for many goods in **pounds sterling**.

TURKISH GOODS

You'll find quite a collection of **carpet shops** around the Temple of

Apollo at Didyma (▶ 100–101). However, some visitors may find the sales tactics of the owners a little overpowering and prices start high so you'll have to be an extremely good haggler to get a bargain here.

Pretty home-made lace and crochet work is on offer at Lake Bafa (▶ 159–161), sold by the ladies who make it or their children. If you stay overnight you'll see the women working on new pieces as they sit out in the warm evening air.

The inland town of **Milas** (between Kuşadası and Bodrum) has the most lively and authentic **market** in the region, which is held every Tuesday.

The town is also renowned for its distinctive **earth-coloured carpets** – available in varying shades of tan, sand and terracotta – and you'll find them on sale at shops located at intervals along the main highway from Kuşadası.

Where to...
Be Entertained

The main cultural events along this coast are linked to the theatre at Ephesus (▶ 87) and the city of İzmir (▶ 72). The İzmir International Festival takes place between mid-June and mid-July, with a host of international classical artists on the programme. For further information and tickets, contact İzmir city tourist office (1344 Sok, 2, Pasaport District tel: 0232 445 7390).

KUŞADASI

Nightlife

Kuşadası has a varied range of evening entertainment. You can take in a Turkish evening featuring belly dancers and folkloric displays at the kervansaray (on the waterfront,

tel: 0256 6144115; www.kusadasihotels.com/caravanesrail). Barlar Sokak or 'Bar Lane' in the old town is where nightlife is concentrated and it gets pretty boisterous in peak season. **Ecstacy** (tel: 0256 612 2208), **Jimmy's Irish Bar** (tel: 0256 612 1318), **Cafe Seyhan** (tel: 0256 614 7985) and **Authentic** (tel: 0256 612 1318) are the most popular – each playing the latest chart sounds until well into the early hours. Kuşadası tourist office is at Liman Caddesi No 13, opposite the harbour entrance (tel: 0256 614 1103).

Waterparks and Boat Trips

If you are tired of tramping around the hot and dusty archaeological sites, head to the slides and rides at **Adaland Waterpark**, at Çam Limanı, 5km (3 miles) north of Kuşadası

(tel: 0256 618 1252; www.adaland.com, open May to October daily) where you'll also be able to swim with the dolphins. South of Kuşadası, another park, **Aqualand**, sits on Long Beach (tel: 0256 633 1252). It is open from May to September, as is **Aquafantasy** at Pamucak Beach (tel: 0232 833 1111).

You can also take day trips to the Greek island of Samos from Kuşadası. The journey takes around 90 minutes and you'll need to book the day before. Tickets are available from agents around the port.

BODRUM

Nightlife

Bodrum's nightlife is legendary with the Disco Halikarnas nightclub on Cumhuriyet Caddesi (▶ 95 and 96) having an international reputation, but you can also find a range of music bars and pubs to enjoy a night on the town. Head to the old town, then later in the evening follow the crowds.

Boat Trips

Day activities tend to centre on the water. The town is a great place for boat trips, either out into the Gulf of Gökova, or to the Greek island of Kós, lying just offshore. A Roman agora and crusader castle are just two attractions in the capital Kós town, which you can explore on foot from the boat dock.

If you'd like to organise your own schedule, you can rent a yacht or gület for a day – or longer if you want. Prices are negotiable, depending on the size and quality of boat, number of people and number of days you want to hire it for.

Novella Yachting have a number of traditional wooden boats. They can be contacted at Cafer Pad'a Cad 55 (tel: 0252 313 2597; for advance information check out www.novellayachting.com).

Bodrum also hosts the **Bodrum Cup** yachting competitions in October. This is your chance to watch the professionals racing on the water.

The Turquoise Coast

Getting Your Bearings

Stretching from Marmaris in the west and skirting around high mountains to Antalya, is a dramatic, varied and unspoilt area known as the Turquoise Coast. Hemmed in by vertiginous peaks and blanketed with virgin pine forest, the coast is still wild. In places, limestone cliffs rise straight from the waves, creating myriad rocky coves lapped by the clear azure water that gives the region its name. Until recently, it was easier to get around by sea than by road and boat trips are still one of the outstanding pleasures of the area.

A single, narrow road weaves up and around the jagged ridges to small resorts strung out along its route. Package tourism has made inroads on the region's edges, but it's far less established at its heart because of the distances from the airports – Antalya to the east and Dalaman to the west. Sailors and independent travellers were prevalent here, and the atmosphere is still a little more laid back than elsewhere along the Turkish Coast.

In ancient times, the Turquoise Coast was the location of ancient Lycia, the final region in Asia Minor to be incorporated into the Roman Empire. The Lycians are thought to have arrived from Crete around 1400 BC, clinging fiercely to their independence and creating a prosperous and stable society. Their legacy remains in their monumental rock tombs, carved into hillside terraces, set upon pedestals or even submerged in the sea. Many dot the landscape, but the best are at Myra and Dalyan.

At the heart of the region beaches are few. The best are at Ölüdeniz, almost a victim of Turkey's tourist boom, and İstuzu (visited on a boat trip along the Dalyan River), which was saved from encroaching concrete because it's a nesting ground of the endangered loggerhead turtle.

Akyak
Taşbükü
400
Marmaris 5
Aktur   Içme
Tur
Sými Bozburun Yarımadası
Ródos   Ródc
Ródos
GR

Lycian tombs carved into the sheer rock face at Dalyan

Kaş, a picturesque resort set around a bay and surrounded by high mountains, is popular with yachtsmen and independent travellers

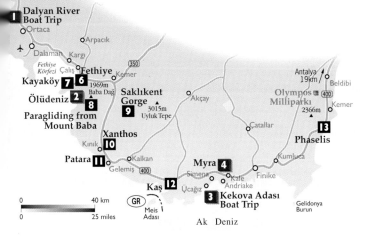

If you thrive on variety, you'll enjoy spending a few days touring the Turquoise Coast. There's plenty to do whether you like lazing on the beach, enjoying watersports, sightseeing from a boat, exploring ancient buildings or admiring wildlife.

The Turquoise Coast in Four Days

Day 1

Morning/Afternoon
Make your way to **1 Dalyan** (➤ 112–113) to catch the 10:30am boat departure for a full day's excursion in the area. You'll take in a river trip (below), tour the ancient site of Kaunos, spend time on the 7km (4-mile) İstuzu Beach, visit therapeutic mud baths and have the chance to swim in a freshwater lake.

Evening
Stroll along the traffic-free main street of Dalyan, then dine at a restaurant along the riverbank and spend the night at a traditional *pansiyon*. Alternatively, head south to **6 Fethiye** (➤ 121) from where it's only a short hop to the places lined up for tomorrow's activities.

Day 2

Morning
Visit the abandoned Greek village of **7 Kayaköy** (➤ 121), in the hills above Fethiye, early in the day. When things start to heat up, head to the beach at **2 Ölüdeniz** (➤ 114–115). If you don't want to bother with beach bar food or walking into town for lunch, take a picnic.

Afternoon
After leaving Ölüdeniz, visit the Lycian tombs that are carved into the hillside above Fethiye. Later on, stroll along the narrow streets of Fethiye for some top-quality shopping before dinner.

Day 3

Morning
Travel south from Fethiye along the 400 coast road to visit the impressive **9 Saklıkent Gorge** (▶ 122) and the ancient city of **10 Xanthos** (▶ 123), and **11 Patara** (▶ 123), which has a 20km (12-mile) turtle-nesting beach. Eat lunch at the village of Gelemiş, near Patara, where you can try traditional *gözleme*, a thin bread stuffed with a variety of fillings, made by the Kurdish ladies who run small restaurants here.

Afternoon
Continue on to the pretty resort of **12 Kaş** (above, ▶ 123–124), taking in the views along the spectacular coast road, with pine-covered hills on one side and sheer drops down to the turquoise sea on the other. Explore the tiny town centre before having dinner at one of its excellent restaurants.

Day 4

Morning
After breakfast, take a switchback ride along the narrow roads through fragrant pine forests to the small village of Üçağız where you can pick up a **3 boat trip to Kekova Adası** (▶ 116–117). Explore the streets of Simena town and its small fort before eating lunch at one of the small cafés there. Later, the boat takes you out into the bay to view the underwater remains of an ancient city submerged by rising water levels.

Afternoon
Drive on to the modern town of Kale (also known as Demre), where you can visit the remains of ancient **4 Myra** (▶ 118–119) just north of the town. Return to the town centre to visit the revered tomb of Noel Baba (Santa Claus) in a Byzantine chapel. There is little to hold you in Myra for the evening, so head east to the coastal resort of Kemer or, better still, on to Antalya (▶ 134–135), about 90 minutes' drive away, for dinner and accommodation.

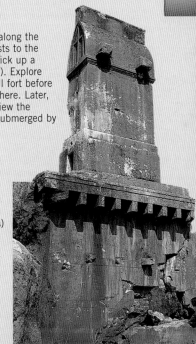

❶ Dalyan River Boat Trip

The Dalyan River trip takes you through freshwater reed beds, shows you bird's eye views of extraordinary Lycian tombs and allows you to explore an ancient city. There's also plenty of time for relaxation, either on a turtle beach or splashing around in therapeutic mud baths. It adds up to one of the most enjoyable and activity filled days you can have along the Turkish coast.

The Dalyan Çayı (Dalyan River) drains Köyceğiz Gölü (Lake Köyceğiz). The river meanders between two high limestone bluffs, its calm waters supporting swathes of reed beds, which provide an excellent environment for birdlife, fish and amphibians.

Quite a Feat

You'll begin your journey at Dalyan village. Just opposite, dramatic **tombs** are carved into the cliffs on the far bank; you'll get your closest view from the boat just after your departure. The tombs are Lycian in style and are probably the finest on the Turquoise Coast, both for their ornate carvings and their improbable location – just how did the 4th-century BC stonemasons work in the middle of this cliff face?

Swamp Things

Ancient **Kaunos** is the next stop on the itinerary. Set on a limestone hill, it offers excellent views over the river delta and

The mud pools at Ilıca are believed to have therapeutic powers

the beach beyond. Despite being one of the least healthy cities in the Roman Empire (malaria was rampant because the surrounding marshes were an ideal breeding ground for mosquitoes) it thrived as a major centre for the slave and salt trades. You can still see a Roman theatre, baths and a *nymphaeum* (monumental fountain), along with a basilica and fortifications from the Byzantine era, but the quality of the remains are far outweighed by the setting. The marshes and reed beds are now home not only to mosquitoes but also to a rich variety of wildlife, including storks, herons, flamingoes, reptiles and tortoises.

Turning Turtle

Your trip continues seaward. The next stop is **İstuzu Beach**, a spectacular 7km (4-mile) swathe of sand, backed by scrub-covered dunes whose western advance threatens to block the river's escape to the sea. İstuzu is a turtle-nesting beach and you may be lucky enough to spot one of these elusive creatures in the water between May and July.

Playing Dirty

Following the stop at İstuzu, the boat retraces its path through the marshes to **Ilıca** for a communal splashabout in the mud baths there. Said to be beneficial for rheumatism and male potency, the baths are just good fun for most people, though the crowds in peak season can get a little overpowering. You can take a shower afterwards and on your return to Dalyan you'll have the opportunity to swim in the cool, fresh water of **Lake Köyceğiz**, home to numerous fish species.

TAKING A BREAK

Dalyan's mellow **Sunray Lounge** (main street, last bar on the right) is a great place to collapse and chill out after your long day. Alternatively, try one of the many riverside fish restaurants.

➕ 183 D2
✉ 65km (40 miles) west of Fethiye
🕐 Daily tours: 10:30, return to Dalyan 4pm
🚌 From Fethiye and Marmaris
💲 Boat trip: expensive; Kaunos: moderate; mud baths: inexpensive

---

DALYAN RIVER BOAT TRIP: INSIDE INFO

Top tips Travel independently to Dalyan and take the boat trip organised by the **Dalyan Cooperative**, which departs from the town dock. These are far less crowded than hired boats used by tour groups, allowing you ample room to see the sights and do a little sunbathing on the deck. You can buy your ticket from the Cooperative's booth beforehand or just turn up if it's not too busy.

• **Take binoculars** for the best views of the tombs and to watch the birdlife on the marshes.

• Although the mosquitoes of Kaunos no longer bring the threat of malaria, they remain a nuisance so bring repellent.

In more depth Between April and September you can view several **pairs of nesting storks** at the Ley-Ley restaurant, 7km (4 miles) out of town towards Fethiye.

2 Ölüdeniz

Ölüdeniz has, without doubt, one of the most beautiful settings in Turkey. Bright golden sands end in a teardrop beach protecting an azure lagoon. This, in turn, is sheltered by a backdrop of fragrant, pine-clad mountains. Ölüdeniz means "dead sea", inspired by the reflections that play across its calm, translucent waters.

This image of pristine nature has been splashed across countless tourist posters and, inevitably, Ölüdeniz came under pressure to cater for the demands of visitors. The balance between development and conservation here remains shaky. Ostensibly a national park, its protective boundary extends only to the attractive western tip of the beach, leaving the eastern section (Belcekız Beach), the narrow valley backing on to it and the plateau above in the hands of developers. The resulting tourist villages – a mishmash of small hotels, *pansiyons* and inexpensive eateries – do not spoil the best parts of Ölüdeniz but it's no longer the virgin wilderness of 30 years ago.

That said, the beach and lagoon are certainly still spectacular; the clear and shallow turquoise water allows sunlight to reflect back from the pebbles on the seabed, resulting in

one of the most photogenic spots along the coast. Early or late in the season you may be able to take in the panorama undisturbed by hordes of other visitors, surrounded only by the sounds of insects and birds.

Active types should head for the eastern section of the beach, which is unrivalled for watersports – skiing and windsurfing – while those in search of more sedate pursuits – snorkelling, canoeing and pedalo rides – will enjoy the western tip of the lagoon.

Parasailing is just one of the many activities that are on offer at Ölüdeniz

TAKING A BREAK

Take a picnic lunch to Ölüdeniz. The cafeteria in the
national park section is poor, and there is little choice in the
resort area. For an evening meal, **Şadirvan** (££), at Ovacik
(5km/3 miles from Ölüdeniz on the Fethiye road), is a local
restaurant specialising in grilled trout and game birds.

🔲 183 E2 ✉ 12km (7 miles) south of Fethiye
🅰 Beach and lagoon: open access; national park: car park May–Oct daily
9–7; Nov–Apr 9–5
🚌 From Fethiye, every 10 minutes from 9–6
🎫 National park: inexpensive; car park: moderate

Tourist Office
✉ İskele Çarşısı No 1, Fethiye ☎ 0252 614 1527

The teardrop-
shaped beach
creates a calm
lagoon, from
which the name
Ölüdeniz,
which means
"dead sea",
derives

ÖLÜDENIZ: INSIDE INFO

Top tips The northern coastline of the lagoon has several **small, sandy beaches**,
in contrast to the pebbles of the outer beach. You can reach these by taking the
lane to the right of the entrance to the national park – you'll find the first
beaches after 1km (0.5 mile), and the furthest 5km (3 miles) down the road.

Hidden gems You can take a **marked footpath** from the northern bank of the
lagoon over the mountains to the deserted village of Kayaköy (▶ 121). If you
are averagely fit, the walk takes about 90 minutes, though there are some steep
sections. There are no refreshment facilities en route, so take water with you.

❸ Kekova Adası Boat Trip

Uninhabited Kekova Adası (Kekova Island) shelters a beautiful strait of pristine waters and numerous islets. Once the exclusive preserve of sailing boats, these waters are now accessible on boat trips from the mainland.

There are two principal starting points for the trip to Kekova. Andriake, near Myra to the east, tends to be popular with large tour groups and is a 40-minute boat journey away across open water. A much better alternative is to leave from Üçağız, a small and pretty fishing village situated on the north shore of the bay. It caters more for independent travellers and, because it takes only 15 minutes to reach Kekova from here, it will give you that much more time for exploring or swimming.

Over the Seas

On departure from Üçağız, look out for the numerous Lycian tombs resting on columns that jut above the waterline. This is **Temiussa,** a large Lycian necropolis. After 15 minutes you'll reach **Kale**, also known as Simena, one of the prettiest and, as yet, least spoiled villages along the

An ancient Lycian tomb rises from the seabed at Kale

Turkish coast (not to be confused with Kale/Demre, ► 118–119). Sturdy wooden jetties offer a berth and, behind the cafés and restaurants lining the seafront, a profusion of rustic, whitewashed houses ascend the hillside. Some have now been converted into carpet shops, but many are still family homes and you'll see chickens and cats scurrying across your path. Local women and children may approach, carrying trays of crochet and lace work or offering guiding services. Crowning the village is a **Byzantine fortress,** built by the Knights of St John (► panel, page 120), from where there are panoramic

views across the gulf and the countryside to the north.

Under the Waves

Back on the boat you'll head past the northern shore of Kekova Island to view **Batikent** (or **Batık Şehir** – Sunken City), which was swallowed up by rising sea levels in the Mediterranean. It's thought to have been a Lycian settlement; look below the water at the tumbledown walls and stacked *pithoi* (large terracotta storage urns) scattered over the seabed. You can't actually get onto Kekova Island, but a small tour boat will take you close enough to see the remains of numerous little square houses built onto its slopes, and an ancient harbour just below the waterline.

TAKING A BREAK

Nearly all boat trips to Kekova stop at Kale around lunchtime. There are some excellent restaurants in the village where you can stop for a snack.

The steep streets of Kale double as a marketplace

🕂 183 F1
✉ 30km (19 miles) east of Kaş
🕐 Boats operate during daylight hours
🚌 To Üçağız; infrequent service from Kaş and Myra
💰 Boat trips: expensive; Castle of St John: inexpensive

KEKOVA ADASI BOAT TRIP: INSIDE INFO

Top tips If you travel by car to Üçağız, watch out for hitch-hikers waiting at the crossroads near the village. They may be **tour boat operators touting for business**.
• To get the best views of the underwater ruins, choose a **glass-bottomed tour boat**.
• Boats trips from Kaş to Kekova are available but take far longer than trips from Andriake and Üçağız, leaving little time to explore once you are there.

In more depth In December 2006 the Turkish government extended the range of protected marine environment as the Kaş-Kekova Specially Protected Area. It cover 3,000ha (7,400 acres) and includes the Patara beach and dunes (▶ 123).
• Andriake has some fascinating and unexcavated **Roman remains**, including the largest ancient granary building in Turkey, dating from the 2nd century AD.

4 Myra

The ancient city of Myra boasts the most accessible Lycian tomb complexes on the Turquoise Coast. Its modern successor, the town of Kale (known to everyone as Demre) is renowned for its close ties with one of the modern world's favourite characters – Santa Claus, St Nicholas, Father Christmas or, as he's known in Turkey, Noel Baba.

Dating back to the 5th century BC, **Myra** was one of the most important Lycian ports. Much of the site remains unexcavated, but its attractions are easy to explore. The main collection of tombs, known as the **Sea Necropolis,** are carved at eye level into the sheer cliff face. You can't go inside but the viewing area gives you the chance to study their finely worked exteriors at close quarters. The theatre next to the tombs is one of the smallest you'll see in Turkey, but it's fairly well preserved, with good views towards the sea from its vaulted *ambulacrum* (upper walkway). Its major decorative element is an **elaborate frieze** of theatrical masks; sections of this are now scattered across the site.

In the 4th century AD, Myra became a Christian bishopric and a local man, Nicholas I, was appointed to the job. He was a man of great piety who was canonised after his death for performing a number of miracles, including resurrecting several children. **Noel Baba Kilesi** (Church of St Nicholas), in the centre of Demre, was inaugurated in his honour in the 8th century and his body placed inside, but it was stolen by pirates in the 11th century. Typically Byzantine in style, the small stone chapel has floors inset with fine marble marquetry and walls adorned with semi-precious stones and frescoes. Those of the Southern Burial Chamber were unveiled again in 2005 after a thorough programme of conservation. A tomb

The Making of Santa Claus

• It's not surprising that St Nicholas is popular – according to legend, his generosity was so great that he threw bags of gold down the chimneys of the poor.

• St Nicholas is the patron saint of children, unmarried women, travellers, merchants, prisoners, Greece and Russia (among others).

• In the 17th century, Dutch immigrants brought their tales of "Sinterklaas" to America. The name was eventually corrupted to become "Santa Claus".

• Because his feast day was celebrated on 6 December, the popular imagination created a man dressed in warm clothing, riding a sleigh – a very practical form of winter transport.

Above: A statue of Noel Baba (St Nicholas), outside Noel Baba Kilesi

attributed to St Nicholas sits in the most southerly aisle, though tests have shown it to be of later date.

TAKING A BREAK

The best bet for *lokanta* meals and substantial snacks is **İpek Restoran** (Gökyazi Mah), a simple and popular eatery on the road to Noel Baba Kilesi.

Left: The Sea Necropolis, a network of Lycian tombs cut into the rock face. The terraces imitate the façades of Lycian houses

Myra
🚩 183 F1 ✉ 3km (2 miles) north of Kale 🕐 May–Oct daily 8:30–6; Nov–Apr 8:30–5 🍽 Cafés by the ticket office (£)
💮 Moderate

Noel Baba Kilesi (Church of St Nicholas)
🚩 183 F1 ✉ Kale centre 🕐 May–Oct daily 8:30–6; Nov–Apr 8:30–5
🚌 To Demre from Antalya and Kaş 💮 Moderate

MYRA: INSIDE INFO

Top tips The church of St Nicholas is protected by an **unsightly plastic roof**, but don't let this put you off. Visit early, before the crowds of tour buses arrive.
• The best time for **photography at Myra** is before mid-morning, when the sun falls directly on the tomb façades.

Hidden gem A lesser known group of tombs, known as the **River Necropolis**, lies only 500m (550 yards) from the main Myra site and were constructed at a similar time to the city. Turn left on the road outside the ticket office and left again at the next junction. The tombs come into view after a couple of minutes' walk, at the base of the cliffs on your left. One in particular – known as the Painted Tomb because of the traces of colour still apparent on the stone – has some fine carved reliefs.

At Your Leisure

5 Marmaris

Marmaris has one of the prettiest settings on the Turkish coast: a wide, sandy bay backed by verdant hills. The old town is a jumble of white-washed cottages and is topped by a diminutive fortress. However, a popular stopover on the Blue Cruise (▶ 95–96) and a package-holiday destination, it has sadly become a victim of its own success. A slew of hotels now back the beach west of the old town and it can be noisy and busy, especially in the height of summer. But it has an excellent range of day boat tours and an exceptional modern marina. The seafront

The picturesque old town and harbourfront at Marmaris

A Day in Greece?

Capital of the Greek island of Rhodes (Ródos), Rhodes is one of the most complete medieval fortified towns in the world. It's an easy day trip from Marmaris, with daily departures from the resort's commercial port (note, you'll need your passport).

In 1309, the "crusading" knights belonging to the Order of the Hospital of St John (the Hospitallers) made Rhodes their headquarters. Originally warrior monks, they became a powerful army, moving from stronghold to stronghold throughout the Mediterranean. In Rhodes, they circled the town with 4km (2.5 miles) of towering walls. Inside, their hospital now houses the Archaeological Museum (open Tue–Sun 8:30–3, admission moderate) and from there, the Street of the Knights, with its 14th-century mansions, leads to the imposing Palace of the Grand Masters (open May–Oct Mon 12:30–7, Tue–Sun 8:30–7; Nov–Apr Tue–Sun 8:30–3, admission expensive).

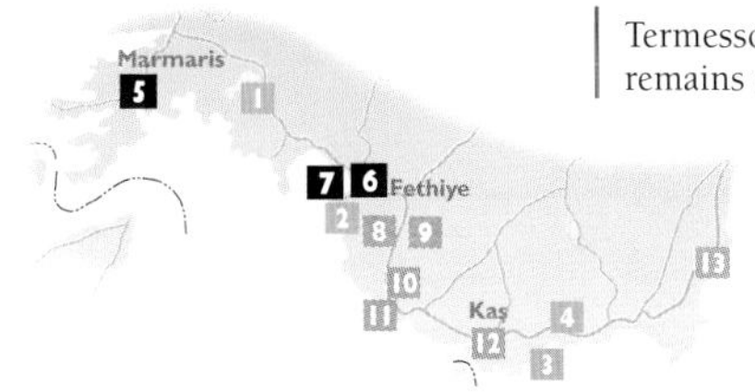

promenade is a great place to let evening turn to night, with a range of bars and restaurants facing the wooden *gülets* bobbing in the harbour. There's also an opportunity to get to the nearby Greek island of Rhodes (➤ panel, page 120).

182 C2

Tourist Office
İskele Meydanı No 2, on the harbourfront ☎ 0252 412 1035 From Bodrum and Fethiye

6 Fethiye

The main town of the Turquoise Coast, Fethiye has no beaches (and therefore no under-dressed bronzers) but it does have a picturesque bazaar and some pretty outdoor restaurants.

As night falls, Fethiye attracts party-goers from Ölüdeniz (➤ 114–115), Hisarönü and Çalış, but the atmosphere is less frenetic than at other resorts.

Nestling in a rocky outcrop at the southern end of a wide bay, Fethiye occupies the site of ancient Termessos. The most obvious remains are a series of Lycian tombs carved into the crag above the town. The largest, the Amyntas Tomb, is one of the most beautiful along the entire Turquoise Coast, its façade fashioned like that of a Greek temple with carved columns and porticoes. Numerous boat trips head out from here for day-long excursions to the 12 islands in Fethiye Körfezi (Fethiye Bay).

183 E2

Tourist Office
İskele Karşısı No 1 ☎ 0252 614 1527 From Marmaris and Antalya

7 Kayaköy

The abandoned medieval settlement of Kayaköy was a thriving Greek village until the mass population exchange between Greece and Turkey in 1923 (➤ 14–15).

The deserted buildings, now resonating only with birdsong, stand on a beautiful hillside overlooking a fertile valley. Some houses have been bought and restored by foreigners and a selection of cafés and tourist shops have sprung up in the lowest reaches, but as you climb higher along the cobbled alleyways the modern world seems very far away. Allow yourself enough time to have a look at the weatherbeaten frescoes inside the church of Panagia Pyrgiotissa on your right, about 400m (440 yards) from the car park.

If you've walked from Ölüdeniz (➤ Inside Info, page 115), the path is marked by dots of browny-red paint on intermittent cornerstones in Kayaköy itself.

183 E2 8km (5 miles) from Fethiye Open access, ticket office May–Oct 9–7; 9–5, rest of year Cafés (£) at the bottom of the village From Fethiye and Ölüdeniz Inexpensive

Amyntas Tomb is the largest of the Lycian tombs at Fethiye

Off the Beaten Track
Take the rural road through the heart of Olympos Milliparkı (Baydağlar Olympos National Park), from Antalya to Kumluca to the south, for magnificent mountainous landscapes, pine forests, small rural villages and panoramic views of the coastline below.

❽ Paragliding from Mount Baba

Always wanted to jump from a mountain peak? Well, here's your chance, albeit with a parachute and a skilled practitioner to guide you back to earth. This is tandem paragliding, and the drop from the summit of Baba Dağ (Mount Baba) to the beach at Ölüdeniz, 1,969m (6,460 feet) below, is said to be the longest in the paragliding world. You'll be rewarded with panoramic views of the forest-clad mountains and sheltered coves of the surrounding coastline, as well as the beach and lagoon of Ölüdeniz itself. Ensure that your insurance covers paragliding, and that you jump with a professionally run company such as Altitude Action (www.altitudeaction.com).

➕ 183 E2 ✉ 7km (4 miles) from Ölüdeniz/12km (7 miles) from Fethiye 💷 Expensive

❾ Saklıkent Gorge

Water-sculpted Saklıkent Gorge is an almost surreal landscape of smooth, high limestone walls twisting along an 18km (11 miles) path into the heart of the Ak Dağlar mountains. With sturdy footwear, the gorge is passable for only 2km (1.25 miles; after this specialist climbing equipment is needed), but this is long enough to appreciate its stark beauty. A metal walkway carries you for the

The entrance to the narrow, water-sculpted Saklıkent Gorge

first 150m (165 yards) to a shady restaurant. Beyond that, you'll need to wade across a torrent issuing from the cliff base to reach the gorge itself. Be prepared: the water is freezing! You can then walk for 15 minutes along the dry gorge bottom.

At the mouth of the gorge there are several restaurants serving fresh trout, which is farmed nearby. Some have tables on wooden verandahs that overhang the river, a perfect place to relax after your walk.

➕ 183 E2 ✉ 50km (31 miles) east of Fethiye, east of the 400 🕐 May–Oct daily 9–7; 9–5, rest of year 🍴 Cafés within and at the mouth of the gorge 💷 Inexpensive

10 Xanthos

One of the most illustrious cities in the ancient Mediterranean – it was even mentioned in Homer's *Iliad* – Xanthos rose to fame again in the 1840s when British explorer Charles Fellows came upon the site. He pillaged its finest relics, including a whole temple, for display in the British Museum in London. Today, however, it's protected as a Unesco World Heritage Site and what's left is in a fairly good state of repair.

Tiers of seats at the theatre at Xanthos

A modern road splits the remains, which are set on a high bluff overlooking the Xanthos valley. Across the road from the ticket office lie a compact theatre, Roman *agora* and a copy of the famed Harpy Tomb, with friezes depicting winged women (harpies) bearing the souls of the dead in the form of children (the original was removed by Fellows). Behind the ticket office, and lost in the wild herb brush, you'll find a Byzantine basilica with mosaic flooring, a Byzantine monastery and a necropolis of Lycian column tombs.

🚊 183 E1 ✉ 63km (39 miles) south-east of Fethiye ⏰ May–Oct daily 8:30–6; 8:30–5 rest of year 🍴 Drinks stall at ticket office 🚌 From Fethiye, Patara or Kaş, passes within 2km (1.25 miles) of the site 💰 Moderate

11 Patara

Along a coastline where almost every square metre of sand has an umbrella planted in it, the 20km (12-mile) beach at Patara is most refreshing. Untouched by developers, Patara's popularity with loggerhead turtles (*Caretta caretta*) has saved it from the concrete. This is one of Turkey's prime turtle-nesting sites and is an official protected natural area. There's just the shore stretching as far as the eye can see.

The ancient city of Patara nestles in fields of dunes behind the waterfront. A Turkish/German archaeological team are currently working on the site throughout the summer season, and there are numerous finds on display in the Antalya Archaeological Museum (► 134–135) – but there's a marvellous theatre and vast 2nd-century granaries waiting to be discovered amongst the tussock grasses.

🚊 183 E1 ✉ 78km (49 miles) east of Fethiye, south off the 400 ⏰ May–Oct daily 9–7; 9–5, rest of year. Beach off limits May–Sep 8pm–8am 🍴 Cold drinks at the beach 🚌 From Fethiye and Kaş 💰 Combined ticket to beach and ancient site: moderate

12 Kaş

This is a delightfully pretty, tiny settlement of narrow cobbled streets and whitewashed Ottoman houses pressed against the water's edge by the Ak Dağlar mountains. At the limits of airport transfer from both Antalya airport to the east and Dalaman airport to the west, and with no beaches nearby, Kaş was one of the last resorts to

attract package tourists, but it offers more bohemian eating and shopping opportunities than many Turkish towns – a legacy of its days as a stop on the hippy trail.

You'll find several Lycian tombs scattered among the streets. These are the only vestiges of ancient Antiphellus, which thrived from the 6th century BC until the Byzantine era. These ancient monuments are often used by local carpet shops as dramatic hanging spaces.

✚ 183 F1 🚌 From Fethiye and Antalya

Tourist Office
✉ Cumhuriyet Meydanı No 5 on the seafront ☎ 0242 836 1238

Traditional Ottoman architecture in the sophisticated resort of Kaş

🔟 Phaselis

The jumble of remains that make up the ancient city of Phaselis don't match up to Ephesus (► 84–87) or Perge (► 136–137), but they're perfect for families or couples who don't see eye to eye about touring archaeological sites. Among the ruins are three wonderful sandy bays where you can leave non-historians to bask in the sunshine, swim or snorkel while you head off to explore the city. It's set among swathes of mature pines – the site is now part of the Olympos Milliparkı (Baydağlar Olympos National Park). The most impressive structure is the Roman aqueduct, of which several sections are clearly visible. A wide, paved avenue links the middle of Phaselis with the southern bay, and it has a small but well

For Kids
• Exploring **Saklıkent Gorge** (► 122) but be careful in the rushing waters.
• Pedalo rides on the **lagoon at Ölüdeniz** (► 114–115) but beware of the sudden drop in depth of Belcekız Beach.
• Rolling in the **mud at Ilıca** on the Dalyan River boat trip (► 113–114).

preserved theatre on its seaward side. Snorkelling just offshore reveals the remains of a harbour in each bay, all lost when the sea level rose.

The area is invaded by families from Antalya at weekends, so if you want some solitude try coming on a weekday.

✚ 185 A2 ✉ 47km (29 miles) south of Antalya on the 400 🕐 May–Oct daily 9–7; 9–5, rest of year
🚌 From Antalya
🎫 Moderate

Where to... Stay

Prices

Expect to pay for two people sharing a double room
£ under US$130   ££ US$130–US$230   £££ more than US$230

MARMARIS

Golden Key Bördubet Hotel ££

In an area where peace is at a premium, this exclusive hotel sits in splendid isolation in an oasis of landscaped watergardens. Guests can take a bicycle or boat out to the private peninsula beach for lazing, swimming and watersports, or spend hours lounging in the gardens. The hotel is a combination of rusticity and trendy sophistication.

🚹 182 C2 ☒ 35km (22 miles) from Marmaris, off the Marmaris–Datça road ☎ 0252 436 9230; fax: 0252 436 9089; www.goldenkeyhotels.com
🕙 Apr–Oct

Pupa Yacht Hotel £

Within 5km (3 miles) of Marmaris' concrete centre, yet on the edge of a frankincense forest, Pupa Yacht has a solid reputation with yachties and landlubbers alike. A little private beach, with good swimming, a yacht anchorage and sunny rooms that take advantage of the sea breezes all contribute to this small hotel's charm. If the tranquillity becomes too much for you, an adjoining taxi rank means that lively Marmaris is only 15 minutes away.

🚹 182 C2 ☒ Adaağız, 48700 Marmaris ☎ 0252 413 3566; fax: 0252 4138 8487; email: hotel@pupa.com.tr; www.pupa.com.tr 🕙 Mid -Mar to mid-Nov

DALYAN

Assyrian Hotel £

Assyrian is a lovely, small resort hotel. Beautifully built from local wood, and with numerous land and water facilities for adults and kids alike, it uses its waterfront location to great effect, and even offers a dozen family apartments. Jump on the free river taxi to the turtle beach and the mud baths (▶ 112–13).

🚹 183 D2 ☒ Maraş Mah, 48840 Dalyan ☎ 0252 284 3232; fax: 0252 284 3244; email: asurotel@super online.com; www.asurotel.com 🕙 Apr–Oct

FETHIYE

Villa Rhapsody £–££

This family owned hotel with 16 rooms in the Kaya Valley, close to Kayaköy, and makes a peaceful retreat after days of exploration. There are walks directly from the entrance into the Turkish country-side. The villa is set in gardens where you'll find the swimming pool with pool bar. The restaurant offers a set lunch and dinner.

🚹 183 E2 ☒ Kayaköy, 48304 Fethiye ☎ 0252 618 0042; fax: 0252 618 0049; www.villarhapsody.com
🕙 All year

ÖLÜDENIZ

Hotel Meri £££

A high-quality family choice, Hotel Meri revels in its lovely private beach and comfortable air-conditioned bedrooms, all of which are purpose built and with splendid sea views. A funicular takes you down to the swimming-pools and lagoon-front restaurant. Full board is only available in season, and bar bills can be weighty, but the Meri's unsurpassed location and charming staff more than compensate.

🚹 183 E2 ☒ Ovacık, 48304, Fethiye ☎ 0252 617 0001; fax: 0252 617 0010; hotel@hotelmeri.com; www.hotelmeri.com 🕙 May–Oct

Where to...
Eat and Drink

Oyster Residences £££

One of the last remaining patrician mansions in the resort, this beautiful hotel has been forged by a professional interior designer. Cool, contemporary Turkish décor gives the whole property a light yet luxurious atmosphere. Rooms have French windows opening out onto generous wooden decks with sumptuous furniture, and there's a cooling pool for guests.

➕ 183 E2 ✉ Belcekız Mevkii 1 Sokak, Ölüdeniz, 48304 Fethiye 📞 0252 617 0765; fax: 0252 617 0764; www.oysterresidences.com 🕒 May–Oct

KAŞ

Hadrian Hotel ££

Situated 5km (3 miles) out of town, the Hadrian clings to peninsular cliffs like a limpet to a rock. The hotel has a luxurious swimming-pool in a spectacular location and steps that lead down to a snorkelling platform. The German/Turkish hosts have hospitality down to a fine art, and their chef is an expert at cooking local fish.

➕ 183 F1 ✉ Çukurbağ Yarımadası 45, 07580 Kaş 📞 0242 836 2856; fax: 0242 836 1387; www.hotel-hadrian.de 🕒 Apr–Oct

KALKAN

Kalkan Regency Hotel ££

This modern multi-level family owned property is set around the pool and offers panoramic views of the Lycian coastline below. Like a large country club, the hotel has a comfortable games room where you can play backgammon or cards, though you are more likely to want to soak in the sun on the deck or your private terrace or balcony.

➕ 183 E1 ✉ Kalamar Yolü, Kalkan, 07960 Antalya 📞 0242 844 2230; fax: 0242 844 3290; www.kalkanregency.com.tr 🕒 May–Oct

MARMARIS

Ney Restaurant ££

Hidden in the warren of streets behind Marmaris' castle (► 120), Ney exemplifies those wonderful restaurants that are a virtuous mixture of excellent, traditional Turkish food, a cramped yet welcoming room and a warm and convivial ambience. It's good value for money but make sure you reserve a table in advance.

➕ 182 C2 ✉ Kale Mah, 26 Sokak 24 📞 0252 412 0212 🕒 Daily noon–4, 6:30–midnight. Reduced hours in winter

Pınarbaşı Restoran ££

One of the oldest restaurants in the Marmaris area, Pınarbaşı is a family run affair with tables scattered amongst verdant, almost tropical, gardens. Trout from local streams is a speciality, there is a good variety of seafood and meat eaters will love the slow cooked lamb. The restaurant has negotiated rates for taxis to bring clients from Marmaris (13km/8 miles away) and return them at the end of the meal.

➕ 182 C2 ✉ Çetibeli Köyü, Marmaris 📞 0252 426 0079 🕒 Mid-Apr to early Nov daily 8am–11pm

DATÇA

Ogun's Place £-££

A family run eatery on the beach-front that's been serving sailors for over 20 years with freshly grilled seafood, *meze* and salads. It's a unpretentious but relaxing place to spend a long lunchtime, and there are rooms of you decide you want to rest longer.

🚩 182 C2 ✉ Mesudiye Köyü, Hayit Buku, Datça ☎ 0252 728 0023; www.ogunsplace.itgo.com ⏰ May–Oct daily 8am–11pm

DALYAN

Sini Restaurant ££

Of the many pretty garden restaurants along the river at Dalyan, Sini is worth a visit for its special Turkish dishes. Try an *al nazik* – mincemeat, eggplant, yogurt and garlic – or *hünkar bağendi* – roast lamb and vegetables on a bed of eggplant with cheese sauce. All the usual Turkish specialities are also available here. You'll eat in the verdant garden under the shade of a century old rubber tree.

🚩 183 D2 ✉ Yali Sokak, Dalyan ☎ 0252 284 2497 ⏰ May–Oct daily 8am–11pm

FETHIYE

Yasmin Bar ££

A hip late-night hang-out, Yasmin Bar plays melodic rock and country-blues music to its young-at-heart clientele. A great location in an ornate building over the Harbour Master's office adds to its attraction.

🚩 183 E2 ✉ On the harbourside, Fethiye ⏰ Apr–Oct daily 7pm–2am

KALKAN

Korsan Marina ££-£££

One of the three restaurants in Kalkan owned by the same family, the Marina is their most up-market establishment, concentrating on excellent national dishes and fresh seafood, though as with many Turkish eateries, the menu is extensive. Located directly on the seafront in the centre of the resort. If you want a simple quick fill-me-up, then the Korsan Kebap, which serves simple grills and remains open all year.

🚩 183 E1 ✉ On the harbourfront, Kalkan ☎ 0533 335 6080; www.korsankalkan.com ⏰ Apr–Oct

KAŞ

Chez Evy ££

Evy is a Frenchwoman who fell in love with Kaş 20 years ago, when it was little more than a fishing village. The town has since fallen madly in love with Evy, whose excellent French cuisine employs the best local ingredients. Her *kalamari* (squid) Provençal is famous all along the coast, and prices are very fair for such good food, so charmingly served.

🚩 183 F1 ✉ Terzi Sokak No 4, Kaş ☎ 0242 836 1253 ⏰ 20 Apr–1 Oct

Café Merhaba £

This combined coffee house and gift shop has become a kind of informal information and meeting place where many travellers stop to recharge their batteries – you can enjoy a good book over your coffee and home made cakes or browse for postcards and souvenirs.

🚩 183 F1 ✉ Ibrahim Serin Caddesi ☎ 0242 836 1883 ⏰ Apr–Oct daily 7am–4pm

ÖLÜ DENIZ

The White Dolphin £££

Owned by the same family as Oyster Residences (▶126). The White Dolphin has built up a reputation as one of the best restaurants in the Fethiye area. The ample terrace offers views across the bay above Ölü Deniz and the menu concentrates on seafood.

🚩 183 E2 ✉ Kidrak Yolü Uzeri 1, Ölü Deniz ☎ 0252 617 0068; fax: 0252 614 1474; www.beyazyunus.com ⏰ Daily 11:30am–11pm

Where to...
Shop

MARMARIS

Marmaris has a scattered bazaar area and is prone to stocking the "cheap and cheerful" **designer copies**, so the better shops really do stand out. The area surrounding Marmaris is famed for its **honey** and you'll see locally produced pots for sale on roadsides as well as more official jars in the shops in town.

FETHIYE

Fethiye is without doubt the best place to shop in this region. It has a very pretty **bazaar** whose streets are shaded by mature vines and it's filled with top-quality **jewellers**, **leather** stores and **handicraft** shops selling original pieces. These are interspersed with some pleasant restaurants so you can have refreshment while you shop.

SAKLIKENT

There is a **carpet co-operative** at Saklıkent village (tel: 0252 636 8790), 3km (2 miles) north of the gorge, where you can learn about the techniques used to produce silk and wool and examine the natural dyes before watching the ladies at the looms. The co-operative also stocks carpets from around Turkey so you'll be able to see a range before you buy.

KAŞ

Kaş still maintains its image as an old hippy hangout on its characterful, though tiny, shopping street. A couple of **collectible and antiques** shops sit cheek by jowl with small designer **jewellers** and more than 15 **carpet stores** (lots of competition though you'll need to haggle to get a good price). **Friday** is market day.

Where to...
Be Entertained

NIGHTLIFE

Evening entertainment on the Turquoise Coast centres mainly on the **bars and restaurants** of the major resorts, catering for the young summer crowd. It's more low key in smaller towns, where the best option is to linger over a meal.

ACTIVITIES AND SPORTS

Boat trips to the islands in the Gulf of Fethiye are extremely popular; tickets are available from the numerous boats in Fethiye's harbour. From Marmaris, you can visit Rhodes (▶ panel, page 120), and there are some pretty day cruises along the Bozburun and Datça peninsulas to the west. From Kaş, you can visit the Greek island of Kastellorizo (Meis).

You may need to leave your passport with the ticket office the day before.

For an **4x4 off-road drive** along the bed of the Eşen River below the Saklıkent Gorge, try **Activities Unlimited** (Hisarönü, Fethiye, tel: 0252 616 6316; www. activities-unlimited-turkey.com). **Compass Yachting** and **Scirocco Travel** (Fethiye, tel: 0252 612 5921; www. compassyachting.com) organise rafting, off-road safaris and diving. The Lycian Way is a marked footpath leading all around the coast.

FESTIVALS

The **grease wrestling competition** at Elmalı is held during the first week in September and the **Ölü Deniz Air Games**, late October, include paragliding and microlighting.

The Mediterranean Coast

Getting Your Bearings

The brooding Taurus Mountains define the contrasting land-scapes of the western Mediterranean Coast. This swathe of 3,000m (9,850-foot) peaks divide the coast from the vast arid Anatolian plain to the north, tempering the northerly winter winds and lengthening the warm summers. In the east, the mountains press against the coast, creating dramatic cliffs and seascapes, and in the west they retreat inland, leaving a wide, flat plain and an almost featureless coastline.

The mountains are also a centre of leisure activity. In the high peaks, summer mountaineering and winter skiing are available for the experienced, while there are great hiking and white-water rafting opportunities in the foothills, most accessible at Köprülü Kanyon.

The ancient Pamphylians made this area their home around 1250BC and, though there are fewer archaeological sites than in the Southern Aegean or the Turquoise Coast, each site stands out either for the quality of its buildings (such as the theatre at Aspendos) or its sheer scale (as at Perge and Side). But it's the predominance of long sandy beaches on the coast that ensure its popularity with holidaymakers from all over Europe.

Capital of the region is the modern and fast-growing city of Antalya, with its pretty old town and dramatic mountain backdrop. Its airport is a major hub for the national and international flights that feed the surrounding holiday resorts. To the east, both Side and Alanya have also grown enormously over the past decade. Though they both have excellent and enduring historical attractions – namely a Roman city and a medieval citadel – most visitors are drawn by the promise of unpretentious holiday fun.

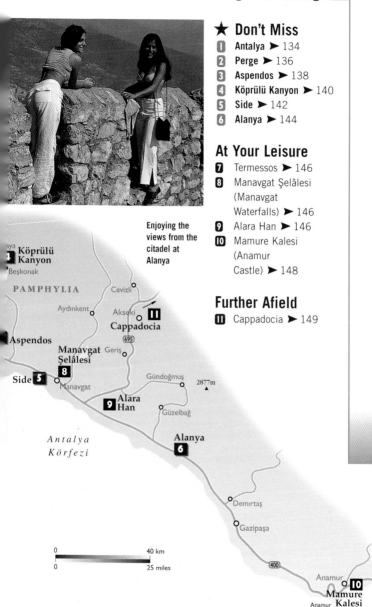

Enjoying the views from the citadel at Alanya

★ Don't Miss

At Your Leisure

Further Afield

Köprülü Kanyon
Beşkonak
PAMPHYLIA
Cevizli
Aydınkent
Akseki
11 Cappadocia
695
Aspendos
Manavgat Şelâlesi
8
Geriş
Gündoğmuş
2877m
Side 5
Manavgat
9 Alara Han
Güzelbağ
Antalya Körfezi
Alanya
6
Demırtaş
Gazipaşa
0   40 km
0   25 miles
400
Anamur
Mamure 10 Kalesi
Anamur Burun

Left: The winding road to Selge, Köprülü Kanyon Milliparkı

Page 129: An exhilarating ride on the waters of Köprülü River

From the city of Antalya, with its dramatic setting, you'll travel into the mountains before making your way east along the coastal plain to explore ancient cities, spending the night at Side. Finally, you'll travel to Alanya with its citadel, and there are numerous outdoor activities to enjoy along the way.

The Mediterranean Coast in Four Days

Day 1

Morning
Head into the hills northwest of **1 Antalya** (▶ 134–135) to the Güllük Dağ Milliparkı (Güllük Mountain National Park), and ruins of ancient **7 Termessos** (▶ 146), set among limestone peaks and draped in fragrant forest. The steep climb from the car park is not for the fainthearted, but once there you can reward yourself with a relaxing picnic lunch under the trees (buy provisions from Antalya).

Afternoon
Return to Antalya for a visit to **Antalya Archaeological Museum** (▶ 134–135). It holds a magnificent collection of artefacts, which were all found at the major sites in the region. Later, explore the narrow streets of Kaleiçi, Antalya's old town set around the harbour, where you can choose somewhere to eat dinner and watch the sunset.

Day 2

Morning
Head east out from Antalya to the impressive remains of ancient **2 Perge** (▶ 136–137) before moving on to the splendid Roman theatre at **3 Aspendos** (▶ 138–139) – both can be viewed in a morning. Have lunch at one of the restaurants alongside the lower River Köprülü near Aspendos.

Afternoon
It's only a short journey west along the 400 from Aspendos to **5 Side** (▶ 142–3), where you can leave the car and explore the combined archaeological remains and town on foot.

Evening
Watch the sun set at a bar on the seafront before picking up a few designer bargains in the busy bazaar; then choose a lively disco to finish your evening. Spend the night at one of Side's hotels.

Day 3

Morning
Have a hearty breakfast before setting out for **4 Köprülü Kanyon**
(► 140–141) and a two-hour river journey by raft or kayak through
spectacular countryside. A healthy and delicious choice for lunch is fresh
trout and salad at a riverside restaurant.

Afternoon
Take to the hills above the rafting bases. The Köprülü Kanyon National
Park protects hectares of beautiful countryside and offers panoramic views
of the valley below. There are also the remains of the ancient city of Selge
to explore. After your exhausting day, return to Side for an early night.

Day 4

Morning
Take the 400 road east along the coast to **6 Alanya** (above, ► 144–145)
where, after checking into your hotel, you can explore the fortified citadel
and the streets of the old town. Have lunch in the citadel.

Afternoon
Enjoy the afternoon sun on the long, curving town beach or visit the
cathedral-like **Damlataş Mağaras** (Damlataş Cave) with its dramatic
stalactites and stalagmites.

Evening
As the sun begins to drop, take a boat trip around the peninsula to enjoy
the view of the citadel from the water and explore the numerous caves
that lie along its waterline.

◖ Antalya

The main city of the Mediterranean coast, Antalya is the fastest-growing conurbation in the country and also one of the most modern and fashionable. Set on a wide bay surrounded by dramatic mountain peaks, its tiny old town, Kaleiçi, has been delightfully restored, and Antalya Archaeological Museum is one of the best in Turkey.

Antalya is more Miami than Med. The stylish, high-rise apartments in its suburbs are set in manicured gardens and serviced by new shopping malls, and there are several huge luxury hotels on the bay. The population is generally young and relatively affluent by Turkish standards, a result of Antalya's status as a busy port and tourist resort.

Kaleiçi

Antalya was founded about 2,000 years ago. By the 16th century, Kaleiçi (meaning "citadel") and its important harbour were surrounded by a wall 5km (3 miles) long. In the Ottoman era, there were four distinct districts housing the Greek, Jewish, Muslim and Mameluke (ruling class) communities, but in the early 1920s foreigners were ordered to leave and the Mamelukes were overthrown (► 17). Kaleiçi sank into slow decline, halted only in the 1980s when a huge restoration programme got underway.

Hadrian's Gate, built in the 2nd century AD, is still the pedestrian entrance to Kaleiçi

The labyrinth of steep, narrow streets and alleyways are still evocative, but renovated mansions now house smart hotels and stylish restaurants. Many have views out across the harbour, now a pleasure marina. The 38m (125-foot) **Yivli Minare** (Fluted Minaret), halfway down the hill, is one of Kaleiçi's major sites. It was built in 1230 by Alâeddin Keykubad, who also designed the Alara Han *kervansary* (► 146–147). Look out also for the triple marble arch of **Hadrian's Gate**, the western point of entry to the old town from modern Antalya, which was built to mark a visit by the eponymous Roman emperor in AD130. After a couple of hours exploring, you'll be ready to have a drink at the harbourside.

Ancient Treasures

Antalya Archaeological Museum lies some 3km (2 miles) out of town to the west. It draws together finds from all the major ancient sites in the region including several Lycian sites along the Turquoise Coast (➤ 107), but the principal collection comes from the city of Perge (➤ 136–137). The most impressive statuary starts at **Gallery 4**, displaying the gods and goddesses that decorated Perge's Hellenistic Gate. At the entrance to the Hall of the Emperors **(Gallery 6)**, you'll be greeted by an exquisite "dancer" carved using two different marbles – her dark hair and flowing gown contrasting with the light marble of her skin. In the gallery, you'll also see a statue of Plancia Magna, whose donations paid for many of Perge's finest monuments (➤ panel, page 137). **Gallery 8** concentrates on Greek Orthodox icons and relics including several relating to Baba Noel (St Nicholas, ➤ 118–119). The museum's climax, however, is **Gallery 14**, where you can see a selection of exquisite friezes from the theatre at Perge. These include scenes of heroic Greek and Roman warriors battling ferocious mermen, depictions of the god Bacchus (patron of theatre and wine), and life-size statues of gods and emperors, who looked down on the audience from the stage wall. The room has been specially decorated to show the carvings at their best; the deep green marble of the floor and walls contrasts well with the pale marble of the figures.

The slender 13th-century Yivli Minare (Fluted Minaret) towers over Kaleiçi

TAKING A BREAK

If you're in town and footsore, head for the restful, shaded gardens in **Karaalioğlu Park**, where tea is served. For larger groups, an entire *samovar* is brought to the table.

➕ 185 A2

Antalya Archaeological Museum
✉ Cumhuriyet Caddesi
🕐 May–Sep Tue–Sun 9–6; Oct–Apr 8:30–12:30
🍴 Café (£) in the museum
🚋 Müze/Liman (Museum/Harbour) line. Tram: westbound to the last stop
💰 Moderate

---

2 Perge

The major Roman city of Perge is the most complete site of its kind along the Mediterranean coast. The remains of many impressive public buildings and its sheer size are testimony to its ancient power. The excavated site is compact but there's ample opportunity to get away from the crowds.

The 2nd-century AD **theatre** is the first building to come into view as you approach, as it sits opposite the ticket office. Once you've parked your car (▶ Inside Info), return here on foot for a closer look. Though not as impressive as the theatre at Aspendos (▶ 138–139), Perge's theatre is renowned for the fine friezes on its stage wall. Many depict images of the god Bacchus (Dionysus to the Greeks), his mythical birth and his youth. He seems to have enjoyed his life – one frieze shows drunken revelry, with the god and his female followers in a wanton ritual frenzy. To the right of the theatre is the **stadium,** a massive sporting arena measuring 234m (256 yards) by 34m (37 yards) and with free-standing terraced seating for 12,000 spectators. The arcades under the terraces housed shops and storage units.

Romantic Ruins

Make your way back from the car park, where you'll find the entrance to the main sections of the city. You'll enter through the **Roman Gate,** a plain wall with a simple entrance, from where you have a good view of the more impressive Hellenistic Gate ahead. Once through the Roman Gate, the remains of the **Roman Baths,** to your left, have been excavated. These show different types of rooms – the frigidarium (cold), tepidarium (warm) and caldarium (hot) – with floors of functional black and white mosaic. Across from the baths is the Roman *agora* (marketplace), dating from the 4th century and forming a perfect 75m (82-yard) square.

The **Hellenistic Gate** is the most striking building at Perge. It's made up of two round, red-brick towers in front of a horseshoe-shaped atrium, which in Roman days was adorned with statues of the gods (now in Antalya Archaeological Museum, ▶ 134–135). The gate leads

Above: The terraces of Perge's stadium could once hold 12,000 people

Left: Paved with marble and flanked by columns, Main Street leads to the Hellenistic Gate

In Grateful Thanks

The tomb of Plancia Magna can be found just outside the Roman Gate. She was the daughter of the governer of the city, and funded many of Perge's most exquisite structures. She became an honorary head priestess, one of several women to hold high office in Perge, which was unusual for the times.

directly to a long colonnaded street, the main thoroughfare. This was cooled and freshened by a deep, water-filled marble channel running along the centre of the road, fed by a monumental fountain at the head of the street. A bridge spans the waterway about halfway along, giving access to the shops on either side. You'll see their mosaic floors and the scant remains of their walls.

🔧 185 B3 ⊠ 15km (9 miles) east of Antalya 🕐 Mon–Sat 8–7
🍴 Drinks vendors near ticket office
🚌 To Aksu from Antalya, then a 2km (1.25-mile) walk
💰 Expensive

PERGE: INSIDE INFO

Top tips The **car park at Perge** actually sits among the remains rather than outside the site. Drive up to the ticket kiosk, which is next to the theatre, and then continue on around the stadium to park the car. To see the stadium and theatre, you must retrace your route for about 300m (330 yards; though there is a footpath shortcut through the stadium) returning to the other side of the car park to reach the Roman gate and the rest of the remains.

• Visit **Antalya Archaeological Museum** (➤ 134–135) to see the wealth of statuary that once decorated the streets, fountains and public buildings in Perge.

In more depth Leave the colonnaded way and head into the tall grasses to the left to find vestiges of many **unexcavated buildings**. Climb the hill behind the monumental fountain to explore the acropolis.

3 Aspendos

The theatre at the ancient city of Aspendos is the most outstanding single monument along the Mediterranean coast. Built during the reign of Roman Emperor Marcus Aurelius (AD 161–180), and renovated after personal intervention by Atatürk in the 1920s, the theatre is in remarkable condition and is still used for concerts.

The theatre makes a striking first impression as you drive into the site car park, and the excellent condition of the high outside stage wall promises much for the interior. You'll enter the theatre through one of the original *parados* (arched vestibules), leading directly into the orchestra floor, which offers an immediate sense of the grand scale of the design. Built in the classic Roman semicircle, the theatre *cavea* (seating area) can accommodate around 20,000 people on 40 rows of seats. Topping the whole structure is an ornate vaulted gallery and wide *ambulacrum* (upper walkway), from where there's an excellent view of the front façade of the stage wall that backs the orchestra floor. Used to support scenery, it was decorated with monumental statuary – many examples can be seen in Antalya Archaeological Museum (► 134–135).

Organised tour groups allow only enough time to visit the theatre, but if you're travelling independently it's worthwhile climbing up the hillside to the plateau behind the theatre. From here there are panoramic views over the whole structure. You'll also see the remains of the rest of the city (the acropolis) to the west, lying forlornly among the tussock grasses. The most impressive building is the basilica, its walls standing some 15m (50 feet) high. If you walk to the southern edge of the plateau you can also see a long and well-preserved section of the city aqueduct, which brought fresh water from the mountains more than 15km (9 miles) away. To walk to the plateau, you'll need stout shoes.

Below: The *ambulacrum* (upper walkway) of the theatre is the site's crowning glory

Left: The theatre set for a modern performance

TAKING A BREAK

In the summer, **Belkıs** (at Belkıs, on the road to Aspendos) is a great place to rest after visiting the ruins. Sit at the outdoor tables and enjoy good, local dishes at bargain prices.

➕ 185 B3 ✉ 45km (28 miles) east of Antalya 🕐 May–Oct daily 9–7; Nov–Apr 9–5
🍴 Snack bar in the car park 💰 Expensive

ASPENDOS: INSIDE INFO

Top tips Touts selling **ancient coins** at a "very special price" are much in evidence at Aspendos. They'll assure you that the coins were discovered at the site but, of course, they are not original – they're simply modern copies given an artificial patina of age. However, if you are not taken in by the sales patter and don't pay way over the odds, they make an interesting souvenir of your visit.

• Some performances of the **Aspendos Opera and Ballet Festival** are staged at the theatre (➤ 154 for details on booking tickets).

4 Köprülü Kanyon

The steeling of muscles; the rhythmical push of oars; the rush of adrenalin; and thousands of litres of foaming water teeming seaward. This is rafting on the Köprülü River. It's energetic but not demanding so it's great for novices, and there's some wonderful countryside to enjoy along the way.

The river snakes down from the foothills of the Taurus Mountains through a canyon – now protected as Köprülü Kanyon Milliparkı (Köprülü Canyon National Park) – and out into a verdant valley. Rafting takes place daily between May and October from just below the canyon exit. You can pre-book a package from Antalya or Side (which includes pick up from your hotel, rafting, lunch and return travel) or make your own way to the canyon and book a ride when you arrive.

To the Gorge

Heading inland off the 400 coast road you'll find the lower bases of several rafting companies where you can leave your car and take their transport onwards. Otherwise, keep the river on your left on your outward journey and after 48km (30 miles) you'll reach the upper rafting station, your departure point. Here you'll be kitted out with wetsuit and helmet and you can choose your boat. The large rafts are great fun and accommodate around 15 people, including a qualified guide. There's a gung-ho atmosphere fostered by team songs and you'll get a souvenir photo for your mantelpiece. Where the rafting starts, pine woodland comes up to the water's edge but as the valley widens out, small farms have sprung up and the fertile soil has been cultivated with corn, cabbages and sesame plants. The valley sides are sheer, some 20m (66 feet) high, gradually reducing in height as you travel towards the sea. There is plenty of time to admire the scenery – that is, when you're not concentrating on trying to negotiate the rapids.

> The churning waters of the Köprülü River, which snakes down through rugged scenery from the Taurus Mountains, in Köprülü Kanyon Milliparkı

Onwards and Upwards

An elegant Roman bridge (left off the main road) marks the upper limit of the rafting stations, and beyond this Köprülü Canyon National Park protects an unspoilt region of pine-clad bluffs heady with the smell of wild herbs. A 13km (8-mile) footpath, just after the bridge, leads into the gorge, but if you want to drive, the road offers panoramic views. After 7km (4 miles) is the village of Altınkaya. Now home to a small farming community, it was the site of ancient Selge. Vestiges of this once-great city remain among the humble cottages, including remains of a theatre and several temples.

On the Water

If this doesn't sound like your kind of thing you can also hire kayaks or canoes for a more sedate ride. The trip lasts between two and four hours including a swim and lunch, which is traditionally grilled freshwater trout by the water's edge.

TAKING A BREAK

There are many restaurants selling freshly grilled trout and soft drinks scattered along the banks of the river where you can stop for a bite to eat after your day's exertions.

✚ 185 B3

Köprülü Kanyon
✉ 48km (30 miles) from the 400 coast road, 96km (60 miles) from Antalya, 74km (46 miles) from Side
🕐 Daily 9–4 (main departures at around 11 and 2)
🍴 Numerous restaurants (££)
💳 Expensive

Mevlana Rafting
✉ Pasha Camii Sok 5, Kaleiçi, Antalya
☎ 0242 243 6950; www.mevlanatour.com

Selge
✚ 185 B3
✉ 55km (34 miles) from the 400 coast road, 7km (4 miles) from the upper rafting stations
🕐 May–Oct daily 8–6; Nov–Apr 8–5
💳 Inexpensive

KÖPRÜLÜ KANYON: INSIDE INFO

Top tips Before taking to the waters, **check your own or the rafting company's insurance** covers both the passengers and the guide on a white-water rafting trip. Although accidents are rare, many holiday insurance companies class it as a dangerous sport and exclude it from their cover.

• The advantage of **travelling to the canyon independently** is that you are free to explore the upper reaches of the national park later in the day. The disadvantage is that you may be waiting some time for others to make up a full boat. If you only want to white-water raft, pre-booking a trip from Side or Antalya, though more expensive, may by the answer.

• If you intend to hike the gorge upstream from the rafting points, or walk the road to Selge, **take plenty of water and perhaps some dried fruit and nuts for energy** as there is nowhere to stop for refreshment along the route.

5 Side

Side is something of a conundrum and is unique along the Turkish coast for being both an ancient archaeological site and a thriving modern holiday resort. That it manages these seemingly divergent roles is noteworthy; that it manages to do it well is remarkable.

Ancient Side was founded on its low, rocky peninsula in the 7th century BC and prospered through trade in slaves, becoming the major port in Pamphylia. Abandoned in the 11th century, the city was reoccupied only in the early 20th century when Muslim fishermen from Crete settled here after the exchange of populations between the Greeks and Turks (➤ 14–15). The long sandy beaches beside the town guaranteed its success as a holiday resort, and now fishing has given way to tourism – with all its associated trappings.

Exploring the City

As you make your way along the only road into town, you'll pass through the **city walls**, from where it's only 500m (550 yards) to the modern town. To your right are vestiges of the colonnaded ancient road that leads to the *agora* on the left. This was the site of the main slave market, the *raison d'être* of the ancient city, but the most interesting artefact here is the remains of a 24-seat latrine, an indication of just how much the Romans embraced communal living!

The Roman baths across the modern road from the *agora* have been converted into **Side Museum** and they now display a selection of fine statuary discovered nearby. The road leads on through the city's original **monumental gateway** (watch for traffic here as the passage is narrow) after which you'll find the public car park on your right and Side's **theatre** on your left. It's unusual to see a totally free-standing arena, as most Greek and Roman theatres were built against hillsides. Inside is another rare feature, a wall around the orchestra built to protect audiences from the wild animals used in gladiatorial contests.

Barriers limit vehicular access to the modern areas of Side, so you're relatively free to stroll around the wide shopping streets that lead down to the harbourside. It's a typical Turkish **bazaar** selling everything from gold and jewellery to leather and carpets, and the shop owners have developed a lively line in banter.

Once you reach the harbour, turn left and after 100m (110 yards) you'll reach the remains of the **Temple of Apollo and Athena.** Five columns and a minuscule amount of entablature have recently been re-erected and these are of exceptionally fine quality, becoming even more beautiful as the setting sun bathes them in golden light.

After 8pm the streets of Side are totally traffic free and as night falls the town gives itself over to modern pleasures. Neon lights flicker into life, music booms out through the still air and the party lasts into the early hours.

TAKING A BREAK

For a hearty meal at the end of the day, try **The End** on Liman Caddesi (➤ 153), a reasonably priced fish restaurant that also has a selection of meat dishes on the menu.

🔲 185 B2

Tourist Office
🖃 Side Yolu Üzeri, 1km (0.5 mile) north of the entrance to town, on the left
☎ 0242 753 1265
🚌 From Antalya and Alanya

Temple of Apollo and Athena
🖃 On the harbourfront
🕐 Open access 🎫 Free

Side Theatre
🖃 At the entrance to the modern town 🕐 Daily 8–6 🎫 Inexpensive

Side Museum
🖃 By the monumental gate
🕐 Tue–Sun 8–6 🎫 Moderate

The elegant columns of the Temple of Apollo and Athena

SIDE: INSIDE INFO

Top tips Don't leave your car on the approach to the town – it will be towed away. Instead, **use the municipal car park** (for a minimal charge).

• Leave some of your sightseeing until the **evening** – both the theatre and the Temple of Apollo and Athena are floodlit at night so you can enjoy them under the ethereal light before you begin to look for somewhere to settle down for dinner.

• A little **tractor bus** links outlying hotels with the centre. It's decorated to look like a train and pulls four or five carriages furnished with long bench seats.

6 Alanya

Alanya's 11km (7 miles) of sandy beaches ensure that the town is a hugely popular package tourist destination. The beaches are split into two wide bays by a titanic crag, 250m (820 feet) high and crowned by a formidable medieval citadel.

There's nothing sophisticated about Alanya. It simply offers holiday fun with its plethora of cafés and restaurants, bars and discos, and designer labels – some authentic – in the shops and bazaars. The new town extends along the coast, with low-rise hotels to the east and west. It has a busy, urban feel and its main thoroughfare, **Damlataş Caddesi**, is "boulevardesque" with its hotels, offices and street cafés. A small area between here and the western harbour is ostensibly traffic free (apart from rebellious motor cyclists) making it a great place to browse.

High Security

Alanya's 13th-century citadel is worth leisurely exploration. With 150 towers and 7km (4 miles) of walls snaking across the hillsides and down to the water's edge, it provided more than ample protection for the garrison and civilians inside. The military headquarters, **İç Kale** (Inner Castle), was built by Selçuk leader Alâeddin Keykubad in 1226 at the summit of the peak, offering breathtaking panoramic views from its crenellated battlements. As you admire the view, spare a thought for the prisoners who used to be thrown from the walls.

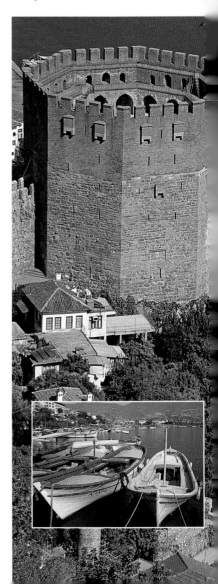

The 13th-century Kızıl Kule (Red Tower) guards Alanya's harbour

Spend some time wandering through the narrow alleyways of **Ehmediye,** a small village of whitewashed buildings lying in İç Kale's shadow, before walking down through the part of the citadel where the civilians lived. Ruined Selçuk buildings swathe the higher slopes below the castle, while near the water's edge is a collection of timber-framed **Ottoman mansions,** many still inhabited. The walk is steep but there are many pretty cafés along the way.

Kızıl Kule (Red Tower) has been guarding Alanya's harbour since 1226. The small folk museum inside is disappointing but the views from the upper platform are certainly not, taking in the variety of pleasure craft that offer trips to the many caves along the waterline. It's best to take these trips in the late afternoon when the sun illuminates the caves' interiors – though the largest, **Damlataş Mağaras** (Cave of the Dripping Stones), a spectacular cavern draped with stalactites and stalagmites, is accessed from land (from the southern end of the western beach) and could easily be seen before you take to the water.

TAKING A BREAK

Numerous attractive **cafés and bars** can be found in Ehmediye below the citadel.

🚩 185 C2 ✉ 137km (85 miles) east of Antalya, 62km (39 miles) east of Side
🚌 From Antalya and Side

Tourist Office
✉ Damlataş Mağarası Yanı, Damlataş Caddesi 1 ☎ 0242 513 1240

İç Kale
✉ At the summit of the citadel 🕐 Apr–Oct Tue–Sun 9–7; Nov–Apr 9–5:50
🍴 Numerous cafés (£) in the citadel 🚌 Hourly from the corner of İşkale Caddesi and Damlataş Caddesi 💷 Moderate

Kızıl Kule (Red Tower)
✉ On the harbourfront 🕐 May–Oct Tue–Sun 8–5:30; Nov–Apr 8–noon, 1:30–5:30 💷 Inexpensive

Cave boat tour
✉ Alanya Harbour 🕐 Daily 9–dusk 💷 Expensive

Damlataş Mağaras
✉ Damlataş Caddesi 🕐 Apr–Oct daily 9–7; Nov–Mar 9–5 💷 Inexpensive

---

ALANYA: INSIDE INFO

Top tips It's a steep, **5km (3-mile) climb** up a winding main road to the citadel. There are refreshments en route, but if the prospect is too daunting, flag down a taxi or *dolmuş*. Or catch a bus from near the tourist information office on Damlataş Caddesi. Buses run hourly on the hour.

• If you take a **taxi** to İç Kale make sure that your driver doesn't drop you at a "friend's café" in Ehmediye instead – it's another 10 minutes' walk to the entrance from here.

• **Visit the citadel in the morning,** firstly because it is cooler, and secondly because the sun is behind you if you want a photo.

At Your Leisure

7 Termessos

The ruins of ancient Termessos would be a major attraction were it not for the difficulty of reaching them. The town sits more than 1,000m (3,280 feet) up in the mountainous Güllük Dağ Milliparkı (Güllük Mountain National Park), north of Antalya. It is so far off the beaten track that even Alexander the Great didn't bother conquering it. The park itself is not serviced by public transport and those who drive to the site independently have a 20-minute climb into the hills from the car park (9km/6 miles from the ticket gate) before reaching the most impressive ruins.

Your efforts will be amply rewarded. Set among rocky crags and surrounded by dense undergrowth, Termessos has probably the most beautiful setting of any ancient city. A mighty archway, Hadrian's Gate, next to the car park, marks the start of your exploration. Take the well-trodden path to the left, once the King's Road, that leads past several separate fortified walls, up to the first plateau, where you'll find the gymnasium and baths (it takes about 20 minutes to reach this point). Climb on for another five minutes to reach a second plateau and the remains of an *agora*, well-preserved *bouleuterion* (city council chamber) and several temples before making your way to the *pièce de résistance*, the theatre (a further five-minute climb). A mountain crag forms a magnificent natural backdrop to the stage, while a gorge to the right leads the eye down to the suburbs of Antalya and the Lycian coastline.

✚ 185 A3 ✉ 27km (17 miles) northwest of Antalya in the Güllük Dağ Milliparkı 🍴 Café at the ticket office 9km (6 miles) from the site 🕐 Apr–Oct daily 8:30–6; Nov–Mar 8:30–5 💰 Moderate

8 Manavgat Şelâlesi (Manavgat Waterfalls)

There are more impressive waterfalls in the world, but the cool air around the 3m (10-foot) cataract offers a contrast to the heat of the coast at Side. Boat trips up the River Manavgat from Side, or a shorter trip from the town of Manavgat, are a popular excursion or you can travel overland by car or *dolmuş*. A rather tacky commercial area has sprung up on the banks at the main falls (signposted "Şelale" from the town) but you can find secluded waterside restaurants and picnic sites upstream if you are travelling under your own steam. It's especially worthwhile if you enjoy riverside landscapes.

Avoid visiting the area at the weekend if you want solitude; the falls and river are popular with exuberant Turkish families from the area nearby.

✚ 185 B2 ✉ 8km (5 miles) northeast of Side 🕐 Apr–Oct daily 9–7; Nov–Mar 9–5 🚌 From Side and Manavgat 💰 Inexpensive

9 Alara Han

A 13th-century Selçuk *han* or *kervansary* (inn for trading caravans)

On Safari

How would you like to leave the tarmac and get off the beaten track in the backwoods of the Mediterranean coast? You can book space on a guided 4x4 safari at Antalya, Side and Alanya. Groups of up to ten open-topped vehicles snake through the countryside for two to three hours, or for the day. A dried-up river normally provides the off-road excitement and you'll explore rural farmland and villages not normally on the tourist itinerary. (► 154 for operators).

Three Top Picnic Spots
• Among the crags and pines at **Termessos** (➤ 146)
• By the crashing waves at the castle at **Anamur** (➤ 148)
• Beside the **Köprülü River** (➤ 140–141)

The trip to Manavgat Şelâlesi is a popular excursion from Side

During the day, Alara Han is a combination of museum illustrating life in the *han*, shop and café. There are good views from the roof bar, taking in the valley and Genoese citadel above. Three nights a week you can enjoy a "Turkish evening" with traditional dancing and food (bookings need to be made at the tourist information office in Antalya, tel: 0242 238 5144). It is expensive but it's a new concept and worth a visit just for that.

🚩 185 C2 ✉ 43km (27 miles) from Side, 39km (24 miles) from Alanya, 5km (3 miles) inland from the main 400 coast road
☎ www.alarahan.com.tr
🕐 Daily 9am–11pm
🍴 On site (£–£££)
💷 Inexpensive; Turkish evening: expensive

at the river crossing of an ancient trade route, Alara Han has been totally refurbished. Uniquely for Turkey, an architectural firm paid for the renovations in return for a lease to run the new attraction. Now you can admire the fortified stone walls with their single large entrance door, allowing access for merchants and their camels, donkeys or horses. Long, simple rooms around the outer walls served as stable blocks (now the restaurant) and at the heart of the *han* several small cell-like rooms were for human guests. The communal courtyard is at the very centre of the *han*, where they would have shared meals and drinks.

For Kids
• Playing pirates at **Anamur castle** (➤ below)
• Rafting on the **Köprülü River** (➤ 140; eight years old or above)
• Going off the beaten track in a **Jeep** (➤ panel, page 146)

Ottoman Empire from the British, who occupied nearby Cyprus. Today, it's popular as a backdrop for Turkish films, with local people tempted in from the fields to be extras.

Three inner courtyards rise within the main walls with a 17th-century mosque taking centre stage in the second. There are views all along the coast from its walls and turrets.

Mamure Kalesi shows its best side for daylight photography in the mornings but is brilliantly illuminated inside and out at night.

➕ 185 D1

Inside the walls of Mamure Kalesi lies a 17th-century mosque

🔟 Mamure Kalesi (Anamur Castle)

The fortress at Anamur, with its towers, moat and crenellated walls, is everything that an archetypal medieval castle should be. The site was first fortified by the Romans in the 3rd century AD and subsequent rulers – a diverse lot, including Armenians, crusaders, Seljuks – all added elements of their own before Anamur took its final form in the early 1400s. The castle was kept in good repair even into the 20th century because it protected the

Tourist Office
✉ Otogar Binası Caddesi ☎ 0324 814 4058 🕐 24 hours, ticket office open daily 8–5:30 🍴 Restaurants (£–££) across the main road 🚌 From Anamur town, which links to Alanya by bus ✋ Inexpensive

Further Afield

⓫ Cappadocia

A whole day's travel separates the coast from Cappadocia but you shouldn't miss this unique region if you're visiting Turkey. It's a landscape of astonishing beauty, shaped by wind and water into hundreds of tall columns called "fairy chimneys". The area also became a refuge for early Christians, who carved hundreds of glorious frescoed churches into the soft rock of the pillars and surrounding hills. These now form one of the most important collections of early-

The landscape of "fairy chimneys" in the Göreme Valley is characteristic of Cappadocia

Christian and Byzantine art in the world, recognised by Unesco as a World Heritage Site.

The heart of the region is the **Göreme Valley**, now a national park containing an open-air museum. A fine example of humans and nature in harmony, it's a microcosm of the region with some fantastic "fairy chimneys" and several fine churches.

The Science Bit

Millions of years ago, Cappadocia was a volcanic region and the durable but thin surface layer of hardened lava or basalt sits on a deep layer of soft porous volcanic rock (tufa). Over millions of years, the basalt has cracked, allowing wind and rain to erode the tufa below. Eventually, the only tufa remaining is that immediately below a basalt "hat", forming a column or "fairy chimney".

You will probably spend three or four hours strolling around the whole area but the best frescoes can be found in **Elmalı Kilise** (Apple Church), **Karanlık Kilise** (Dark Church), and the **Tokalı Kilise** (Buckle Church), which is outside the museum boundary but part of the same ticket.

Only 3km (2 miles) north of here is another open-air museum, this time in several dips at **Zelve Valley**. A magnificent troglodyte monastery complex is carved into the rock of the horseshoe-shaped first basin. The religious community here thrived from the 9th to the 12th centuries, and its extensive interior chambers were still family homes as late as the mid-20th century.

A 65m (213-foot) rocky peak some 4km (2.5 miles) southwest of Göreme, **Üçhisar** also has a labyrinth of connected man-made caverns. The panorama from the top is worth the difficult climb, but for the less adventurous, views of the rock from the old Greek village surrounding it are equally rewarding.

As you travel through the region you'll see that the cones and columns are not obsolete. Many among the verdant crops – which provide grapes for the famed Cappadocia wines – are still used as family homes or store-houses. This, as much as the protected sites, makes Cappadocia special.

🚏 186 A4
🚌 From all major towns in Turkey (with transfers) to local transport hubs at Nevşehir and Ürgüp

Göreme Open-Air Museum
🚏 186 B4 ✉ 2km (1.25 miles) from Göreme village 🕐 Daily 8:30–7
🚍 To Göreme village 💷 Expensive

Zelve Open-Air Museum
🚏 186 B4 ✉ 3km (2 miles) from Göreme village 🕐 Daily 8:30–7
🚍 To Göreme village 💷 Moderate

Travelling in Cappadocia

There are good value three-day **bus tours** from all the main resorts along the south coast – it's whistle-stop, but you'll see the main sights. Some operators offer five-day packages from the Aegean coast but much of this is taken up with extra travelling. Independent travellers face a 9am to 7pm drive from the Mediterranean coast; longer from the Aegean.
• **Walking in Cappadocia** is the best way to get to know the region. Hire a guide in Göreme so you don't get lost (try **Hiro Tour** at the bus station, tel: 0384 271 2542).
• A **balloon flight** is a great way to view the landscape. **Cloud 9** (50108 Nevşehir tel: 0384 271 2442; www.cappadociaballoons.com) organises four-hour trips featuring one hour aloft.
• The lush, verdant **Ilhara Valley**, 70km (44 miles) southwest of the Göreme region, is stunning and has many rock chapels cut into the valley walls between the villages of Belisırma and Ilhara.

Where to... Stay

Prices

Expect to pay for two people sharing a double room
£ under US$130   ££ US$130–US$230   £££ more than US$230

ANTALYA

Hotel Alp Paşa £

This classy old mansion on Hesapçi Sokak in the heart of Kaleiçi (Antalya's old town) has been well-restored, complete with antiques, into a smart hotel. Rooms have an individual feel, some have Jacuzzis. There's also a tiny swimming-pool and an excellent restaurant.

➕ 185 A2 ✉ Hesapçi Sokak No 30, Kaleiçi, Antalya ☎ 0242 247 5676; fax: 0242 248 5074; www.alppasa.com ☺ All year

Sheraton Antalya Voyager ££

If you're in need of sumptuous pampering, look no further than this futuristic resort, situated at Konyaalti beach. Run with unusual efficiency, the Voyager has gorgeous gardens, a pool with a waterfall and a stunning beach just five minutes' walk away. Staying here is expensive, to be sure, but everything is as it should be, and conforming to the Sheraton standards has not dimmed the charm of the Turkish management and staff.

➕ 185 A2 ✉ Yil Bulvari, 07050 Antalya ☎ 0242 249 4949; fax: 0242 249 4901; reservations.voyager@ starwoodhotels.com ☺ All year

Atelya Art Hotel £

The steep, narrow streets and alleyways of Kaleiçi, Antalya's old town, however charming, can feel stifling in summer, which makes this *pansiyon* feel all the more refreshing. Atelya's plain exterior opens into a jasmine-scented patio courtyard, and the building has been sensitively restored. Rooms are clean, comfortable and airy (even without air-conditioning), and there's a small restaurant. A newer, slightly more stylish annexe is across the alley. To reach the hotel, follow signs for Hotel Alp Paşa.

➕ 185 A2 ✉ Barbaros Mah, Civelek Sokak 21, Kaleiçi, Antalya ☎ 0242 241 6416; fax: 0212 241 2848; www.atelyahotel.com ☺ All year

Doğan Hotel £

First established as a *pansiyon* nearly 20 years ago, Doğan is now a fully-fledged hotel that fills three tastefully converted historic houses in Antalya's Kaleiçi. Rooms are air-conditioned and very comfortable; the best ones overlook Doğan's gorgeous garden with its scented shrubs, small swimming-pool and tinkling water feature. Top-floor rooms also delight in a good view of the harbour.

➕ 185 A2 ✉ Memerli Banyo S No 5, Kaleiçi 07100, Antalya ☎ 0242 241 8842/247 4654; fax: 0242 247 4006; www.doganhotel.com ☺ All year

SIDE

Turquoise Hotel ££

If your wallet can stand it, and you don't want to visit Side itself, choose the Turquoise Hotel, 3km (2 miles) out of town. Lavish luxury is yours, as is a forest-fringed compound, filled with pools and bars, and even a polo ground. With a 200m (220-yard) private beach, this is a self-contained resort from which you need never stray.

➕ 185 B2 ✉ Sorgun Mevki, Side ☎ 0242 756 9330; fax: 0242 756 9345; www.turquoise.com.tr ☺ All year

Where to...
Eat and Drink

Prices

Expect to pay for a three-course meal, excluding drinks

£ under US$15   ££ US$15–US$25   £££ more than US$25

ANTALYA

Dönerciler Çaşısı £

This busy intersection has lots of cheap döner and pide stalls and it's known locally as the "döner market". You'll be surrounded by Turkish families, students and courting couples, so it's a great place to strike up a conversation with the locals. No stall really stands out but it's the stop for a quick cheap and tasty lunch during your sightseeing trip.

🚹 185 A4 🖂 Corner of Cumhuriyet and Atatürk Caddesi 🕓 Daily 8am–1am

Gül ££

This Turkish/German owned restaurant has a loyal local and ex-pat clientele and it is fast becoming popular with visitors. The menu offers traditional local dishes that are well cooked and not overpriced. Food is served in the shady garden, which offers a respite from the often busy streets of Kaleiçi.

🚹 185 A2 🖂 Kocatepe Sok 1, Kaleiçi 🕿 0242 247 5126 🕓 Daily 11am–midnight

Kral Sofrası £££

Kral means "king", and indeed, this restaurant is the king of all

with kitchenettes. The hotel has two restaurants and a range of snack bars. The hotel is contracted through the TUI group.

🚹 185 C2 🖂 Konaki, 07490 Alanya 🕿 0242 510 0000; fax: 0242 565 1531; www.paschabay.com.tr 🕓 All year

CAPPADOCIA

Yunak Evleri £££

This exceptional property combines six original cave houses in a natural amphitheatre, plus a fine 19th-century Greek stone mansion. The 30 rooms reflect the long history of the region and are furnished with local antiques and fine carpets in Ottoman style, each with a CD player (the mansion holds a store of CDs to borrow). Every room has a patio with countryside views

🚹 186 A4 🖂 Yunak Mahallesi, 50400 Ürgüp 🕿 0384 341 6920; fax: 0384 341 6924; www.yunak.com 🕓 All year

Hane ££

A comparatively inexpensive beach hotel, Hane has much to recommend it. Its beach is clean, as are its air-conditioned rooms, and there's even a pleasant park in which to spend a leisurely afternoon just sitting or enjoying a drink. The hotel provides plenty of activities and watersports facilities for guests, and the lively town Side, with more eating, drinking and dancing possibilities, is about 6km (4 miles) away.

🚹 185 B2 🖂 Kumköy Mevkii, 6km (4 miles) from Side 🕿 0242 756 0413; fax: 0242 756 0417; www.hanehotels.com 🕓 All year

ALANYA

Pascha Bay Hotel ££

This is an excellent resort property, perfect for family holidays. There is a very large swimming pool, plus the beachfront and the sea to enjoy. Rooms are bright and colourful

Antalya's seafood establishments. The fish on offer is always bright-eyed and fresh and cooked by experienced staff, although the service can at times be rather off-hand. You can expect to pay handsomely for the privilege of eating here but you will enjoy every mouthful, especially if you're offered a dish of sweet, succulent, grilled prawns.

185 A2 ⊠ Old Harbour, Kaleiçi, Antalya ☎ 0242 241 2198 ⓒ Daily 11:30–11

Restaurant Hasanağa £

Hasanağa offers food to fill out your waistband at prices that hardly lighten the wallet. Here you can enjoy all that's best in traditional Turkish cuisine, including an amazing mezze display and excellent stuffed squid. If you're finding the service a touch unsympathetic, have the waiter explain a dish that intrigues you. He'll be pleased at the interest you show and might even offer you an off-menu speciality, such as grilled kılıç (swordfish), if it's in season.

185 A2 ⊠ Mescit Sokak 15 (next to İmaret Camii), Antalya ☎ 0242 247 1313 ⓒ Daily 11:30–10:30

SIDE

Ayışığı ££

The name means Moonlight in Turkish and as the name suggests this is an open-air restaurant where you eat by candlelight on the water's edge or in the verdant garden – perfect for a romantic meal – but by no means limited to couples. The menu has fish and a range of European options, plus a good range of tasty Turkish hot and cold meze dishes.

185 B2 ⊠ Barbaros Caddesi 49 ☎ 0242 753 1400 ⓒ May–Oct daily 11am–1am

The End ££

Typically of Turkish fish restaurants, The End invites you to choose the catch of the day from where it reposes on its refrigerated display. Unusually, however, The End is as comfortable cooking meat as fish, and does a roaring trade in Osmanlı kebab (beef blanketed in garlicky tomato sauce, then topped with cheese), which is great if your digestion is up to it. If you fancy lobster you can expect to pay royally but otherwise The End is good value.

185 B2 ⊠ Liman Caddesi, Side ⓒ Daily, continuous service throughout the day

ALANYA

Eski Ev ££

One of Alanya's most longstanding restaurants, Eski Ev offers tasty Turkish cuisine in pretty surroundings, with tables set in the garden of the old house that gives the restaurant its name. You are more likely to be sat among Turkish diners who know good food, rather then masses of tourists. Eski Ev is also a café, so you can visit throughout the day for a refreshing cup of tea, coffee and some Turkish snacks. It supplies a shady interlude to a hot day of sightseeing or bargaining at the market.

185 C2 ⊠ Dalmataş Caddesi 44 ☎ 0242 511 6054 ⓒ Daily 11am–11pm

Red Tower Brewery Restaurant ££

Since 2004, Red Tower has been brewing its own beer, one of the few micro-breweries in Turkey. In addition to great beers – light pilsner, golden helles, darker marzten and weizen wheat beer – the Brewery is an American style diner with great snacks like burgers, plus a range of Turkish cuisine. Come here for a refreshing drink or make time for a full dinner.

185 C2 ⊠ İskele Caddesi 80 ☎ 0242 513 6664; www.redtowerbrewery.com ⓒ Daily 11am–1am

Where to...
Shop

ANTALYA

Kaleiçi (▶ 134), Antalya's picturesque old town quarter, has some very stylish carpet shops interspersed with cheaper souvenir shops and is a good place to browse. The **bazaar**, directly across Cumhuriyet Caddesi from the old town (exit Kaleiçi by the clock tower to the west) is filled with souvenirs and T-shirts. For modern boutiques, try the main thoroughfares of **Ismet Paşa Caddesi and Atatürk Caddesi** (which skirts the walls of Kaleiçi on the eastern flank).

SIDE

Side has an excellent, bustling shopping area abounding with jewellers and some good leather shops, with a smattering of designer copies. There is a **carpet co-operative** on the main road 15km (9 miles) west of Side (Anadolu Carpet Belkis Beldesi, Serik, tel: 0242 735 7483) where you are introduced to carpet weaving techniques before you buy: there's no obligation to part with your money if you just want to look.

ALANYA

There is a good choice of shops but the shopping area, off **Damlataş Caddesi** towards the harbour and around the bus station, is not as picturesque as at Side and you have to search harder for genuine Turkish produce. For lace and table linen, both hand- and machine-made, head for **Ehmediye village** in the citadel.

ALARA HAN

Alara Han *kervansary* (▶ 146–147) sells a range of well-sourced **original items** such as *kilims*, clothing and hand-worked pottery.

Where to...
Be Entertained

CULTURAL FESTIVALS

Antalya is the hub of cultural activity, often in conjunction with the theatre at Aspendos. It hosts the **Antalya Film Festival**, in October. In June, the **Aspendos Opera and Ballet festival** runs an international and an experimental programme. Demand for tickets is high; for the avant-garde programme you might get tickets from the theatre or tourist office on the day. Contact the Antalya office of the Tourist Board (tel: 0242 238 5144) for advance bookings. **Alara Han** holds regular folkloric evenings (▶ 146–147).

OUTDOOR ACTIVITIES

For outdoor activities, from rafting to mountaineering, try **Kesit Tourism and Travel Agency** (Narenciye Caddesi 7/4, tel: 0242 322 1414; www.kesit.com) in Antaly. Check that operatives have insurance for any sporting activity, as your travel insurance probably won't cover you.

Antalya has a large watersports complex at the BeachPark recreation area west of the city.

AquaLand (tel. 0242 249 0900; www.beachpark.com.tr) has slides and other water based rides. The neighbouring **DolphinLand** (contact details as for AquaLand) offers the chance to swim with these intelligent sea mammals.

Further east are two water parks at Manavgat, outside Side. **Water Planet** (tel: 0242 527 5165 www.waterplanet.ccm.tr) and **Club Alibey Aquapark** (te: 0372 948 7622; www.clubalibeymanavgat.com.tr).

Walks and Tours

1 OLD ISTANBUL

Walk

This walk gives you the chance to experience the authentic hubbub of the city without wandering too far from its main attractions. It also provides the opportunity to explore the legacies of Istanbul's Byzantine and Ottoman history.

DISTANCE 4.5km (3 miles) **TIME** 5 hours (including visits to attractions)
START POINT Hipodrom, Sultanahmet district ✚ 179 C2
END POINT The waterfront at Eminönü ✚ 179 C3

1–2

The **Hipodrom** (Hippodrome) was the grand stadium of Constantinople. Originally a Roman chariot-racing arena, it was adapted by the Byzantines to hold 100,000 people. The structure was destroyed during the crusades and today only its outline remains. It's now a shady ornamental garden, bordered by Sultanahmet Camii (the Blue Mosque) on one side and the Türk ve İslam Eserleri Müzesi (Museum of Turkish and Islamic Art, ▶ 51) on the other.

From the three ancient obelisks to the south of the

gardens, walk north until you meet the bottom of **Divan Yolu Caddesi**, the main artery and tram route of the Beyazıt district.

2–3

Cross the street and head left. After some 300m (330 yards), you'll find an ornate white marble building flanked by a small cemetery

of large and impressive Ottoman tombs. This is the *türbe* (tomb) of Sultan Mahmud II, who died in 1838. Then, turn right out of the entrance and continue down Divan Yolu. **Cennet**, a traditional-style café selling Turkish snacks, is

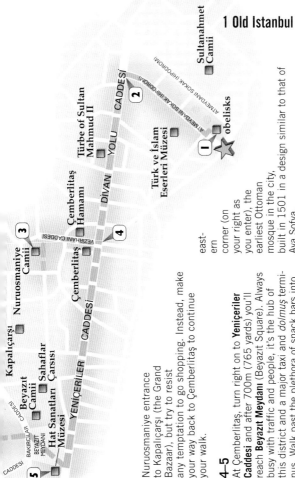

200m (220 yards) further on. It's a little kitsch, but Turks as well as tourists enjoy the good-quality food on offer.

Further down Divan Yolu, you may notice the tram stop at Çemberlitaş before you see the monument there. **Çemberlitaş** ("the hooped stone") is the column erected by Emperor Constantine when he made Constantinople the capital of the Roman Empire in AD330. The copper hoops that give the column its modern Turkish name were added a century later to bolster it against earthquakes. It was charred by the huge fire that consumed this part of the city in 1779, and now suffers further humiliation as a roost for hundreds of pigeons. Take a right turn at Çemberlitaş Square (look out for the entrance of the 16th-century Çemberlitaş Hamamı on your right; ▶ 21) to reach **Nuruosmaniye Camii**, commissioned by Sultan Mahmut I in 1748.

3–4
The mosque is notable for its decoration, which is a departure from classical Islamic lines because it incorporates baroque and rococo features. Walk through the shady courtyard of the mosque to reach the Nuruosmaniye entrance to Kapalıçarşı (the Grand Bazaar), but try to resist any temptation to go shopping. Instead, make your way back to Çemberlitaş to continue your walk.

4–5
At Çemberlitaş, turn right on to **Yeniçeriler Caddesi** and after 700m (765 yards) you'll reach **Beyazıt Meydanı** (Beyazıt Square). Always busy with traffic and people, it's the hub of this district and a major taxi and *dolmuş* terminus. Walk past the plethora of snack bars into the relative open space of the square itself – there's a huge, crowded Saturday market here. The square is anchored by **Beyazıt Camii** on its eastern corner (on your right as you enter), the earliest Ottoman mosque in the city, built in 1501 in a design similar to that of Aya Sofya.

Behind the mosque is **Sahaflar Çarşısı**, the old secondhand book market (▶ 59) and across the square to the west (walk parallel

Meydanı. Built on the site of the original Ottoman palace of Mehmet the Conqueror, its main building, erected in 1866, was the Ottoman Ministry of War. It became a university in the 1920s when ministries were moved to Ankara, the new Turkish capital. Walk through the ornate entrance gate and the campus, where you'll see Turkish students in both Western and Islamic dress. Opposite the far gate you will find **Süleymaniye Camii** (▶ 53). Visit the mosque and then, if you feel hungry, try delicious Ottoman-style dishes at **Darüzziyafe** on Şifane Caddesi, housed in part of the mosque complex.

The campus is closed at weekends, so if it's a Saturday or Sunday take Besim Omer Pasa Caddesi, the first road to the left of the compound, and turn right at Süleymaniye Caddesi to reach **Süleymaniye Mosque**.

6–7

From here, head downhill through one of the oldest parts of Istanbul, a maze of streets that was once the commercial heart of Byzantium. Still replete with tiny workshops, it's usually crowded with Istanbullu going about their daily business, and you'll be dodging handcarts and bulging shopping bags. Look up from the storefronts to the

original vaulted stone arcades above. These are at least 600 years old.

The most direct route through the district is along Sami Onar Caddesi and **Ismetiye Caddesi** (stretching east from the southeastern corner of Süleymaniye Mosque). At the crossroads with Uzunçarşı Caddesi, carry straight on and take a left at Sabuncu Hanı Sokak, which will lead directly to the rear of **Mısır Çarşısı** (the Egyptian Bazaar, ▶ 52). Turn left here, then right at the corner of the bazaar before taking the first left (Hasircilar Caddesi) to reach diminutive **Rüstem Paşa Camii**, a mosque set incongruously above a row of shops. Designed by Sinan, architect of Süleymaniye Camii, and built in 1561, it is one of the most beautifully decorated in the city, graced by thousands of Iznik tiles.

7–8

Walk back through the U-shaped Egyptian Bazaar to one of its two front entrances and on across **Yeni Camii Meydanı**. Yeni means "new", and it is one of the later imperial mosques, having been completed in the 1660s. On the far side of the square is an underpass that leads beyond a four-lane highway to the waterfront and ferry terminals at **Eminönü**, where this walk ends.

Left: Book trader at Sahaflar Çarşısı, the secondhand book market

with Yeniçeriler Caddesi) is **Hat Sanatları Müzesi** (the Museum of Calligraphy), housed in an old *medrese*. The small collection includes rare copies of the Koran and ornate sections of Ottoman Arabic manuscripts. Open Tuesdays and Wednesdays only.

5–6

The campus of **Istanbul University** (Istanbul Üniversitesi) is to the north of Beyazıt

2 BAFA GÖLÜ AND HERACLEIA
Drive

DISTANCE 105km (65 miles)
TIME 6–8 hours (including site tours)
START POINT Kuşadası ✠ 182 B3
END POINT Kapıkırı (Heracleia) ✠ 182 B3

Bafa Gölü (Lake Bafa) was created when the Latmos Gulf was cut off from the sea by the silting of the River Menderes. Heading here from the resort of Kuşadası (▶ 97) gives you the chance to view the Turkey of another era. The region has been inhabited for more than 3,000 years and donkeys and horses still outnumber cars. It's also a chance to replace the pop music of beach bars with the sounds of crows and buzzing insects.

1–2
Take the D515 south from Kuşadası in the direction of Söke. As you leave behind the ever expanding suburbs of the resort behind you, the hills of the Dilek Peninsula (▶ 97–98) come into view ahead with the Greek island of Sámos only a few kilometres offshore to the west. You'll pass through rolling countryside of olive groves and corn fields.

2–3
At **Söke**, follow the signs for Bodrum. Take the ring road to avoid the town centre, because there is nothing here that merits a visit and road conditions are poor. As you head out of town (1.5km/1 mile along the Bodrum road) look out for a bright green **mosque** on your right.

3–4
Just beyond the mosque, take the right turning signposted for Priene and Milet (Miletos). From here the landscape becomes much more rural. The flat delta of the **River Menderes**, or Meander (whose wandering path gave the word "meander" to several languages) spreads out to your left. Two crops predominate: cotton and sunflowers. During the summer, there are views of hectares of golden blooms while September and October are the months of the cotton harvest. Just

Harvesting cotton from the fields in the flat delta of River Menderes

beyond, through the village of **Güllübahçe**, is the right turning for Priene (▶ 98–99) where the 2,500-year-old city's lower remains can just be seen from the roadside.

distance what looks like a hill. This is what remains of **Milet** (Miletos, ▶ 99–100), one of Turkey's great ancient cities, which was suffocated by mud from the river.

5–6

Take the left turning at the sign for Miletos even if you don't want to stop and tour the whole site. This short side road will lead directly to Miletos' greatest structure, the **theatre**, and on past the faded grandeur of **İlyas Bey Camii** (İlyas Bey Mosque). It is well worth taking 15 minutes to explore this 15th-century place of worship; the elaborate marble *mihrab* suggests that it has seen better times. Then rejoin the main high-way and remember to turn left at the intersection of the main road to continue your journey.

6–7

When you reach the village of Akköy, you can either take the route directly ahead to **Didim** (ancient Didyma and Temple of Apollo, ▶ 100–101), which is one-way-in, one-way-out, or you can miss out this section of the drive altogether and go directly to ...

and flamingos as well as for native herons and egrets. The whole region has been desig-nated a protected area, the **Dilek Yarımadası/Büyük Menderes Deltası Milliparkı.**
At 55km (34 miles) from Kuşadası you'll cross the Menderes itself. As you do, you'll see in the middle

Rural life seems unchanged at Bafa Gölü (Lake Bafa)

4–5

After driving 9km (6 miles) from Güllübahçe, take the left turn at the sign for Didim (Didyma), which will take you south across the delta. Out towards the sea on your right are vast salt flats that provide an important environ-ment for migratory birds such as storks

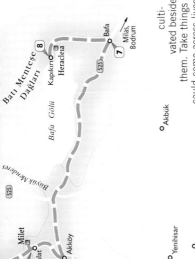

A sea of sunflowers in the Menderes delta

turning left in the direction of Milas.
At the intersection of the B525, turn right
(signposted Milas/Bodrum). The road immediately begins to ascend through forested hills.
A vast residential area is being planned at the
top of the first climb; here you'll get your first
view of **Lake Bafa** on your left. The road skirts
the western shore of the lake for several
kilometres, offering stunning views of small
islands with Byzantine remains, the far bank
and the Batı Menteşe mountain range behind.

7–8

The village of **Bafa** is 5km (3 miles) beyond
the point where the road leaves the lakeside.
You'll take a left turn here (signposted
Kapıkırı) from where it is 10km (6 miles) to
your journey's end. The route from Bafa to the
lake is a boulder-strewn landscape dotted with
small farms. Cowsheds and stables are built
against these vast rocks, and small fields are
culti-
vated beside
them. Take things slowly here as you
could come across livestock around any bend.

The village of **Kapıkırı** sits among the
ancient stones of Heracleia, whose remains
top the peaks and lie under the waters of the
lake. The city was founded in the 5th century
BC and reached its zenith during the
Hellenistic era but suffered from the silting
that caused problems for other ancient cities
in the region. Very few buildings have been
professionally excavated and they are scattered and hidden in the undergrowth. A visit
would be best made with a village guide.

3 OLYMPOS TO THE CHIMAERA

Walk

The natural flames of Chimaera have been burning since ancient times, imbuing this region with magical aura – this was the home of the gods.

The walk to Chimaera from ancient Olympos takes you through some of Turkey's most typical landscapes, including a long, sandy beach and high, pine-clad mountains. This very southern tip of the Turquoise Coast, now part of the Olympos Beydağları National Park, is separated from the main road by dramatic mountain ridges and until recently was a tourist-free backwater. Nowadays, you won't be on your own in the summer, as Olympos is a popular spot for boat trips from the resort of Kemer further up the coast, but out of season it's a world apart.

To reach the start of the walk take the sign for Olympos marked "Olympos 11/Adrasan (Çavuşköy) 15" from the main 400 road. Take

DISTANCE 14km (9 miles) **TIME** 4 hours (including site visits)
START POINT Ancient Olympos 🚩 185 A1
END POINT Chimaera (return to Olympos to pick up your car) 🚩 185 A2

care, as there are two turnings very close to one another. From the intersection you'll get fine views of the mountain ridges ahead. Leave your car at the Olympos car park and buy a ticket (if the office is manned) before you go in.

1–2

Begin your walk by taking the main route through the ancient site. Olympos, a Lycian city, is set on freshwater stream in a narrow gorge. There are numerous unexcavated remains among the lush vegetation; the most obvious are long warehouses sitting by the water's edge. Hidden in the grass is the monumental marble door of a now-lost temple (follow the sign "Mabet" left from the main path) so it's your chance to feel as if you're on a voyage of discovery. Look out for birds, insects and reptiles such as lizards, turtles

The monumental door of the Mabet temple, hidden among high grasses at Olympos

and frogs, as Olympos is a rich environment for many species. The main deity of Olympos was Hephaistos, god of fire and blacksmiths – it's not surprising given its proximity to the Chimaera flames.

2–3

You'll emerge from the gorge directly onto Olympos beach, one of the most impressive on the coast, and relatively undisturbed because it's a turtle-nesting site. The sand stretches several kilometres ahead and is halted only by a ridge of cliffs jutting out into the sea. Walk along the top of the beach until you reach the Yavuz Pansiyon.

Signs on the Lycian Way

3–4

From here, head 100m (110 yards) inland across the Olympos beach car park and a river-bed (1.5km/1 mile from Olympos site) into the village of Çıralı, which has small restaurants and bars, some of them on the beach. This is also a good place for stocking up on water for the onward journey. You'll go past here on the return journey too, when you'll probably need a cooling drink.

4–5

At Çıralı you'll see yellow signs towards "Chimaira" (note the different spelling). Turn right when you reach the main road, then walk on through the village and past a mosque on your right.

5–6

You'll pass small farmsteads and citrus groves until, after 2km (1.25 miles), a dirt road forks off to the left (marked by another yellow sign). From here you walk for 20 minutes, ever closer to the surrounding mountain ridges. "Base camp" for the final ascent is the Chimaera car park (ticket office: daily 9–7, Apr–Oct; 9–5, rest of year; access to the site is possible outside these hours). There's also a refreshment vendor, and if you don't have any water buy some here, despite the expensive prices, because you'll need it later on.

6–7

A 30-minute, steep climb brings you out to the first set of flames. The route is very obvious but some sections are slippery with gravel and there are tree roots and rocks to catch your feet.

In ancient times, the glow of the flames could be seen from far out to sea and sailors believed that the fire was emitted by a fire-breathing dragon called Chimaera. Around 30 flames flicker their way out and over the rocks, the highest leaping about 50cm (20 inches) above the ground. Not all are easily seen, so watch your ankles as you clamber about and be careful where you put your hands. There is a gassy smell quite close to the flames but it's not strong enough to make you queasy.

The flames are at their most romantic as night falls. They are also easier to see as the skies darken and some visitors have an almost spiritual experience at this time. But if you do stay after dark remember that you will be returning down steep narrow path-ways, so it's imperative to take a torch, or engage the services of a guide.

7–8

Return down the mountain and back to the paved road. Rather than returning to Çıralı the way you came, turn left from here and com-plete the loop by walking along the beach road or, for wonderful views of the mountains, along the beach itself. You'll reach it in about 10 minutes (1.5km/1 mile), from where its 2km (1.25 miles) to the village or 3.5km (2 miles) to the beach entrance to Olympos.

Swimming in the freshwater stream around which the ancient city of Olympos was built

Left: The flames at Chimaera are caused by natural gases escaping from the bare, rocky landscape

4 THE ELMALI

Drive

DISTANCE 235km (146 miles) **TIME** 8 hours (including site visits)
START POINT Kaş ⊞ 183 F1
END POINT Kaş ⊞ 183 F1

The route towards the town of Elmali takes you to some of the least visited parts of the Turquoise Coast. You'll travel over the fringe of peaks that press against the coast, and into a caldera-like valley, then climb again over a higher mountain range until you reach the wide and fertile Elmali plain. The landscape is totally different from the waterside.

You'll need a four-wheel drive vehicle to reach the Green Lake and nervous drivers – and passengers – may want to give this a miss, but otherwise the roads are suitable for a normal rental car.

1–2

Take the main **400 coastal highway** east out of Kaş towards Antalya. You'll climb steeply up the hillside that presses the resort to the coast. Look to your right for panoramic views of the surrounding coastline – there are a couple of parking places for you to get out for a longer view or to take photographs.

2–3

After 11km (7 miles), take the second turning at the roundabout, following the route signposted "Elmali/Antalya" and you'll immediately begin to descend through fragrant pine forest on a series of tight zigzags. You'll also get a good view of a wide plain stretching out ahead. In the valley bottom, around the village of **Kasaba**, is arable land that's at its best from May to June, when the wheat ripens and is harvested. Later in the year, the ground is left fallow and herds of goats search out the last remaining morsels.

After 37km (23 miles), the road climbs up into the **Ak Dağlar** mountains proper. The pines change from lowland to upland species and you'll drive into the winter snowline over the 1,560-foot (5,120-foot) **Karaovabeli Geçit** (Kurova Pass). From here you can look ahead to the

Elmali means "the place of the apples" and the wide plain just outside the town is planted with many orchards

3–4

After about 52km (32 miles) you'll pass a reservoir in the valley bottom, and after 60km (37 miles) you should turn left into **Gömbe** if you want to take on the challenge of reaching the Green Lake (▶ panel, page 167). This diversion is suitable for four-wheel drive vehicles only.

4–5

Continue on the main road, heading towards **Elmalı**. The wide plain outside the town is filled with orchards. Elmalı means "the place of apples", and, depending on the time of year, your journey could be filled with fragrant blossom (May) or offer a close view of the harvest (October). If you do travel later in the year,

The façade of 17th-century Ömerpaşa Camii in Elmalı

mighty, barren face of **Uyluk Dağ** at 3,015m (9,890 feet), its summit covered in snow even in early summer. In the valley, look at the poplar trees lining the fields and riverbanks as you travel north to the village of Gömbe.

apples falling from the back of heavily laden lorries – they're weighty enough to do some damage to your car.

5–6

About 23km (14 miles) from Gömbe, the road meets the intersection of the 635 road. Take a left and it's then 7km (4 miles) to Elmali itself. Make your way through the newer sections of town to the old town, which is in the shadow of Elmali Dağ (Elmali Mountain), and park near the 17th-century Ömerpaşa Camii (Ömerpaşa Mosque) so that you can walk around the old town to the north. The cobbled streets lead to numerous Ottoman houses, most still used as family homes. You may be the subject of some friendly interest from locals, especially children, who don't see many tourists. Visit Elmali during the first week in September and you'll discover the Turkish Wrestling Festival in full swing. The competition dates back over 600 years and competitors travel from across the country in the hope of winning the title.

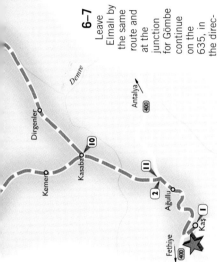

6–7

Leave Elmali by the same route and at the junction for Gömbe continue on the 635, in the direction of Finike/Kaş. About 20km (12 miles) from Elmali, the road leaves the plain over the Avlanbeli Geçit (Avlan Pass).

7–8

After 34km (21 miles), you'll reach the village of **Arif**. Watch for the left turn on a series of

Diversion to Green Lake

If you have a four-wheel drive vehicle, you can make the 15km (9-mile) diversion from Gömbe to **Girdev Gölü** (Green Lake).

Take the Gömbe road past the river bridge that leads into the centre of town (about 2km (1.25 miles) from the last junction). You'll travel past a colourful mosque on the right just before entering the town itself. About 1km (0.5 mile) after the bridge, the road splits. Take the right-hand fork and you'll climb up past several farms until the tarmac stops after a further 2km (1.25 miles). From here, it's another 10km (6 miles) to the lakeside, as the road takes you up the side of a treeless valley on dirt and stone roads. It's a dramatic landscape of scree slopes and a great test of your driving skills.

When the lake holds water the reflections of the mountains and sky are inspirational but it's not a true lake and can be totally dry in late summer. Small, sturdy huts sit around the shoreline. Until a couple of generations ago, these were used by shepherds who came up with their flocks from Gömbe to spend the summer.

although the theatre and early-Christian basilica are among the remains on higher terraces.

8–9
Return to the main road and continue south for 4km (2.5 miles), where there is a right turn that takes you back to Kaş.

9–10
You'll travel on through eroded limestone rocks to **Yazırbeli Geçit** (Yazır Pass), at 850m (2,790 feet), where goats will probably be your only company. The road has some uneven surfaces but these pose no problems for an ordinary vehicle. From here the valley pans out in front – a landscape blanketed with greenhouses growing ubiquitous tomatoes. Eventually, after 46km (29 miles), you'll reach Kasaba once again.

10–11
Turn left at the village intersection for your return journey up and over the mountains to the roundabout. Then take the second turning on the right, which takes you down along the coast and back into Kaş.

The tortuous route up to Girdev Gölü (Green Lake) is suitable only for four-wheel drive vehicles

The ruins at Arykanda, in a dramatic hillside setting surrounded by high peaks

tight bends to the ancient site of **Arykanda**, 100m (110 yards) from the intersection. Arykanda's setting, 750m (2,460 feet) above the valley bottom and surrounded by peaks of more than 3,000m (9,850 feet), makes it worth a visit, though you may find the views more impressive than the remains. There has been a settlement here for nearly 4,000 years but Arykanda reached its zenith from 200BC until the early days of Christianity, after it joined the Lycian Federation. The lower acropolis contains the most obvious buildings,

Practicalities

GETTING ADVANCE INFORMATION

Websites
www.tourismturkey.org
www.kultur.gov.tr

In the US
Turkish Embassy Info
Counsellor's Office
2525 Massachusetts Ave
Washington DC 20036
☎ 202/612-6800

Turkish Tourist Office
821 United Nations Plaza
New York NY 10017
☎ 212/687-2194

BEFORE YOU GO

WHAT YOU NEED

		UK	Germany	USA	Canada	Australia	Ireland	Netherlands	Spain
● Required ○ Suggested ▲ Not required △ Not applicable	Some countries require a passport to remain valid for at least six months beyond the date of entry – contact their consulate or embassy or your travel agent for details.								
Passport/National Identity Card		●	●	●	●	●	●	●	●
Visa		●	▲	●	▲	▲	●	●	●
Onward or Return Ticket		○	○	○	○	○	○	○	○
Health Inoculations (tetanus and polio)		▲	▲	▲	▲	▲	▲	▲	▲
Health Documentation (► 174, Health)		△	△	△	△	△	△	△	△
Travel Insurance		●	●	●	●	●	●	●	●
Driving Licence (national) for car rental		●	●	●	●	●	●	●	●
Car Insurance Certificate (if using own car)		●	●	△	△	△	●	●	●
Car Registration Document (if using own car)		●	●	△	△	△	●	●	●

WHEN TO GO

Temperatures based on the West Coast of Turkey

High season   Low season

JAN	FEB	MAR	APR	MAY	JUN	JUL	AUG	SEP	OCT	NOV	DEC
13°C	14°C	17°C	21°C	25°C	30°C	34°C	34°C	31°C	26°C	19°C	14°C
55°F	57°F	63°F	70°F	77°F	86°F	93°F	93°F	88°F	79°F	66°F	57°F

☀ Sun   ☁ Cloud   Wet and Windy   Sun/Showers

Temperatures are the **average daily maximium** for each month. The Turkish coast has a long tourist season running from the start of April to the end of October. Both the beginning and the end of the season have milder temperatures and the chance of showers, but offer the opportunity to lie on beaches and tour the sights without hoards of fellow travellers. However, frequency of trips such as white-water rafting (► 140–141) and jeep safaris (► 146, 154) may be lower due to lack of demand.

In high summer (late June to early September), the temperatures can rise to more than 30°C (86°F), with Istanbul and Cappadocia both becoming very hot. This is a popular time for European holidaymakers in all the coastal resorts, when facilities can become stretched and tourist attractions crowded.

GETTING THERE

By Air Istanbul's Atatürk International Airport is the main gateway into Turkey for scheduled flights, although there are a small number of flights to İzmir and Antalya.

From the UK Flying time to Istanbul is three hours; to İzmir and the airports of the southeast around three and a half hours. Major airlines include Turkish Airlines and British Airways (who both fly direct), KLM, Air France, Lufthansa and Alitalia (with connections in Europe).

From the rest of Europe Flying time from central Europe is around two and a half hours. Major carriers include Turkish Airlines, KLM, Air France, Lufthansa and Alitalia.

From the US and Canada Flying time from North America's east coast is at least ten hours. Major carriers are Turkish Airlines who flight share with American Airlines and British Airways (with stopover in the UK).

From Australia Turkish Airlines operate flights to Singapore, Hong Kong and Bangkok for connecting flights from Australia and New Zealand. It may make more sense to fly direct to a major European hub such as London or Amsterdam for connecting flights to Turkey. Carriers include Qantas, Air New Zealand and British Airways.

Ticket prices Prices are highest between April and October, but by shopping around and booking ahead you can lower the cost. Last-minute deals can also save money. Holiday packages (combining air fare, hotel room and some meals) can offer good value for money and are very popular from the UK and mainland Europe. Companies offering packages include Thomson and Airtours and JMC. For an independent pre-booked itinerary contact a specialist travel agent.

By car The best way to drive to Turkey is by ferry from Italy (Venice, Ancona, Brindisi or Bari) either to Greece (Igoumenitsa or Patras) for an onward drive to Turkey, or directly to Turkey (Çeşme in the summer or İzmir). Customs officials require proof of vehicle ownership and will issue a temporary certificate of importation, which must be surrendered when you leave.

TIME

 Turkey is two hours ahead of Greenwich Mean Time (GMT) but operates daylight saving from late March to late October, when clocks are three hours ahead of GMT.

CURRENCY AND FOREIGN EXCHANGE

Currency The unit of Turkish currency is the Turkish lira (YTL). On 1 January, 2005 the currency was devalued and new notes and coins were issued. One New Turkish lira (YTL) is equivalent to 1,000,000 old Turkish lira. Notes are in denominations of 1, 5, 10, 20, 50 and 100 lira. One lira comprises 100 kurus. Coins come in denominations of 1, 5, 10, 25 and 50 kurus, and 1 lira). Do not accept old Turkish Lira notes in change. These should now be out of circulation.

Exchange Banks and exchange offices charge a commission of up to 4 per cent. Travellers' cheques are difficult to exchange outside the main resorts; it's best to have them from a major name such as Thomas Cook or American Express. There are ATMs in resorts and main towns, where you can withdraw cash using a cirrus card/credit card and a PIN number. Your bank will charge a small fee.

Practicalities 171

TIME DIFFERENCES

GMT
12 noon

Turkey
2pm

USA New York
7am

Germany
1pm

Spain
1pm

Australia
12 midnight

WHEN YOU ARE THERE

CLOTHING SIZES

UK	Turkey	USA	
36	46	36	Suits
38	48	38	
40	50	40	
42	52	42	
44	54	44	
46	56	46	
7	41	8	Shoes
7.5	42	8.5	
8.5	43	9.5	
9.5	44	10.5	
10.5	45	11.5	
11	46	12	
14.5	37	14.5	Shirts
15	38	15	
15.5	39/40	15.5	
16	41	16	
16.5	42	16.5	
17	43	17	
8	36	6	Dresses
10	38	8	
12	40	10	
14	42	12	
16	44	14	
18	46	16	
4.5	38	6	Shoes
5	38	6.5	
5.5	39	7	
6	39	7.5	
6.5	40	8	
7	41	8.5	

NATIONAL HOLIDAYS

1 Jan	New Year's Day
23 Apr	National Independence and Children's Day
19 May	Atatürk Commemoration, and Youth and Sports Day
30 Aug	Victory Day
29 Oct	Republic Day

Moveable holidays
Islamic holidays are also observed in most of Turkey, although they do not affect opening hours (see below). The dates change from year to year, but, as a guide, the month of Ramazan (Ramadan) begins around .2 September in 2008. Contact the Turkish Tourist Office (► 170–171) for confirmation of dates.

OPENING HOURS

○ Shops
● Offices
● Banks
● Main Post Offices
● Museums/Monuments
● Pharmacies

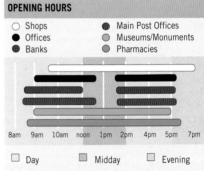

8am 9am 10am noon 1pm 2pm 4pm 5pm 7pm

□ Day   ▨ Midday   □ Evening

Shops Shops are often open daily until at least 10pm in tourist resorts.
Banks Banks are closed at the weekend.
Post Offices Major post offices are open Monday to Saturday from 8am to midnight and from 9 to 7 on Sunday. Local post offices usually close for an hour at lunchtime, and all day Sunday.
Museums/Monuments Museums are closed on Mondays. Most archaeological sites are open daily from 8:30–6 in summer and 8:30–5 in winter.
As Turkey is officially a secular country, opening hours are not affected by Ramadan as they are in Muslim countries.

POLICE	155
TRAFFIC POLICE	154
GENDARMARIE	156
FIRE 110 (FOREST FIRE ALERT 177)	
AMBULANCE	112

PERSONAL SAFETY

Turkey is one of the safest countries to visit, but petty crime is on the increase, especially in tourist areas, so take the following precautions:

• Put all valuables in the hotel safe
• Do not carry more cash than you need
• Leave nothing on view in vehicles or on the beach
• Walk only in well-lit streets at night
• Take only official taxis

Police officers wear blue uniforms. In addition to the usual police officers, there are special tourist police in major resorts who should be able to speak some English and/or German.

Police assistance:
☎ **155** from any phone

TELEPHONES

major resorts will allow international direct dial calls made with phone cards or credit cards. If you have difficulty, major post offices have the facility for operator calls that you pay for after the call has been completed.

**International Dialling Codes
Dial 00 followed by**

Public phones only accept cards (available at post offices, press kiosks and some general stores). Newer public phones in Istanbul and the	**UK**	44
	USA / Canada	1
	Irish Republic	353
	Australia	61
	New Zealand	64
	Germany	49
	Spain	34

POST

Post offices
Signposted "PTT" or "Post Office" on a yellow banner, post offices can be found in each city or resort. They also offer telephone facilities, and some larger offices offer exchange facilities. **Post boxes** are also yellow. In addition, **stamps** are usually available where postcards are sold.

ELECTRICITY

The power supply is 220 volts, as in mainland Europe. However, there are regular interruptions to the supply. Sockets take two-round-pin plugs but there are two sizes in use. Bring your own adaptor. Visitors from the US and Canada will need a transformer.

TIPS/GRATUITIES

Tips are always appreciated and never automatically added to your bill. As a general guide:

Restaurants	10 per cent
Bar service	small change
Taxis	10 per cent
Tour guides	10 per cent
Chambermaids	1YTL per day
Porters	1YTL
Cloakroom/lavatory attendants	small change

UK
☎ 0212 334
6400

USA
☎ 0212 335
9000

Ireland
☎ 0212 259
6979

Australia
☎ 0212 243
1333

New Zealand
☎ 0212 244
0272

HEALTH

 Insurance There are no reciprocal health arrangements, so you are strongly advised to include health and accident cover in your travel insurance. If you plan to take part in sports such as white-water rafting (▶ 140–141) or paragliding (▶ 122), make sure you are specifically covered for it.

 Dental services Dental treatment must be paid for, so make sure that your travel insurance includes dental treatment. You will have to pay for the service and claim it back later, so obtain a receipt. Most dentists speak some English, and your hotel should be able to recommend a local practitioner.

 Weather The sun is strong in Turkey, especially in the summer (July to September are hottest), with an average of 12 hours of sunshine a day. Always wear a strong sun block, and take a hat and covering layer (perhaps a long-sleeved shirt) and sunglasses when sightseeing or at the beach. Avoid the midday sun.

 Drugs Pharmacies (*ezcane*) can be found in every town and resort and are a good place to go for advice on minor ailments such as sunburn and upset stomachs. They can sell a range of drugs over the counter, including antibiotics. Private hospitals are for the most part clean and modern, though they tend to be small.

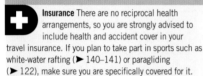 **Safe Water** In towns and resorts, the tap water is safe to drink but can be heavily chlorinated and does not taste good. It's better to drink bottled water, which is cheap and universally available, either still (*memba suyu*) or fizzy (*maden suyu*).

CONCESSIONS

Children Many hotels offer reductions for children and all historical sites offer discounted prices.
Students Carry an international student card for reductions at museums and archaeological sites. InterRail passes are available to European citizens under 26 and cover the rail networks in Turkey as well as mainland Europe, though the network isn't comprehensive.
Senior Citizens There are few concessions for senior citizens either for travel or for entry into attractions.

TRAVELLING WITH A DISABILITY

Turkey does not cater well for visitors with disabilities. Always enquire with hotels about facilities before booking. Modern museums will have ramps but most archaeological sites do not and are difficult to navigate if your mobility is limited.

CHILDREN

Children are made very welcome in Turkey and they'll be fussed over in bars and restaurants. Though few have special menus for young appetites, adult portions in Turkey are fairly small. Only the largest resort hotels offer a children's club.

LAVATORIES

Public facilities can be found in museums and at archaeological sites, for which there will be a small charge. Restaurants and bars will have facilities but not all will have a supply of lavatory paper, so carry tissues just in case. Away from the main towns and resort areas, lavatories may be of the "hole in the floor" variety.

CUSTOMS

The import of wildlife souvenirs from rare and endangered species may be either illegal or require a special permit. Before buying, check your home country's customs regulations.

SURVIVAL PHRASES

Yes (formal) **Evet**
No **Hayır**
Hello (formal) **Merhaba**
Goodbye (formal) **Güle güle/Allaha
ısmarladık**
How are you? **Nasılsınız, iyi misiniz?**
Please **Lütfen**
Thank you (very much) **Çok teşekkür
ederim**
Excuse me **Özür dilerim**
I'm sorry **Çok üzgünüm**
You're welcome **Bir şey değil**
Do you have something…? **Daha...bir
şeyiniz yok mu?**
How much? **Ne kadar?**
I'd like **Istiyordum**

OTHER USEFUL WORDS & PHRASES

Good morning, madam/sir
   Günaydın hanmefendi/beyefendi
Good afternoon **İyi günler**
Good evening **İyi akşamlar**
Good night **İyi geceler**
Fine, thank you **Teşekkür ederim**
Very well **Çok iyiyim, teşekkür
ederim**
I think so **Zannederim**
I'm not too bad **İdare eder**
Cheers! **Şerefe!**
What's your name? **Adınız ne?**
Who? **Kim?**
What? **Niçin?**
When? **Ne zaman?**
Why? **Niçin?**
How? **Nasıl?**
How much? **Ne kadar?**
Open **Açmak**
Closed **Kapalı**

DIRECTIONS

Where is…? **... nerede?**
   - the beach **Plaj ne nerede?**
   - the bank **Banka ne nerede?**
   - the bus stop **Otobüs durağı ne
      nerede?**
   - the post office **Postane ne
      nerede?**
   - the hospital **Hastane ne
      nerede?**
   - the hotel **Otel ne nerede?**
   - the sea **Deniz ne nerede?**
   - the telephone
   - the lavatory **Tuvalet ne nerede?**
Left **Sola**
Right **Sağa**
Straight ahead **Doğru**

IF YOU NEED HELP

Help! **İmdat!**
Could you help me, please? **Bana yardım
   eder misiniz?**
Do you speak English? **İngilizce
   konuşmasını biliyor musunuz?**
I don't speak Turkish **Türkçe konuşmasını
   bilmiyorum**
Could you call/fetch a doctor quickly,
please? **Hemem bir doktor çağırır mısınız
   lütfen?**
Could I use your telephone? **Telefonunuzu
   kullanabilir miyim?**
Police **Polisi**
Ambulance **Ambülans**

TRAVEL

Airport **Havaalanı**
Harbour **Liman**
Bus station **Otogar**
Bus stop **Otobüs durağı**
Bus **Otobüs**   Taxi **Taksi**

NUMBERS

0 **sıfır**	12 **on iki**	30 **otuz**	120 **yüz yirmi**
1 **bır**	13 **on üç**	31 **otuz bır**	200 **iki yüz**
2 **iki**	14 **on dört**	32 **otuz iki**	300 **üç yüz**
3 **üç**	15 **on beş**		400 **dört yüz**
4 **dört**	16 **on altı**	40 **kırk**	
5 **beş**	17 **on yedi**	50 **elli**	500 **beş yüz**
6 **altı**	18 **on sekiz**	60 **altmış**	600 **altı yüz**
7 **yedi**	19 **on dokuz**	70 **yetmiş**	700 **yedi yüz**
8 **sekiz**	20 **yirmi**	80 **seksen**	800 **sekiz yüz**
9 **dokuz**		90 **doksan**	900 **dokuz yüz**
10 **on**	21 **yirmi**	100 **yüz**	
11 **on bır**	22 **yirmi bır**	110 **yüz on**	1,000 **bin**

EATING OUT

I'd like to book a table for seven o'clock please **Saat yedi için bir masa ayırtabilir miyim?**

I'd like a table for two, please **İki kişilik bir masa lütfen**

We've/we haven't booked **Yer ayırtmıştık (ayırtmamıştık)**

Can we wait for a table? **Boş bir masa için bekleyebilir miyiz?**

Do we have to wait long? **Çok beklememiz gerekiyor mu?**

Could we sit here/there? **Buraya/oraya oturabilir miyiz?**

Can we eat outside? **Dışarıda da yiyebilir miyiz?**

Do you have a menu in English? **İngilizce yemek listeniz var mı?**

Could we see the menu/wine list? **Yemek listesini/şarap listesini rica edebilir miyim?**

Could I have the bill please? **Hesap lütfen?**

THE MENU

alkollü içkiler alcoholic drinks
alkolsüz içkiler non-alcoholic drinks
aperatif aperitif
balık çeşitleri choice of fish dishes
çorba çeşitleri choice of soups
etli yemekler meat dishes
etsiz yemekler vegetarian dishes
ızgara grills
kahvaltı breakfast
KDV dahil including VAT
menü menu
meyva fruit
mezeler starters
salatalar salads
şarap listesi wine list
sebze yemekleri vegetable dishes
servis dahil service included
servis hariç service not included
sıcak yemekler hot dishes
soğuk yemekler cold dishes
tatlılar sweets (puddings)

---

alabalık trout
armut pear
ayran yoghurt drink
ayşe kadın fasulyesi green beans
bakla broad beans
baklava sticky pastry
balık fish
barbunya mullet
beyaz şarap white wine
bezelye peas
biber peppers
biftek steak
bira beer
bisküvi biscuits/ cookies
böbrek kidneys
börek fried pastry
burghul bulgar/ cracked wheat
cacık cucumber and yoghurt
çay tea
çerkez chicken
ceviz walnut
ciğer liver
çikolata chocolate
çilek strawberries
çoban mixed
çorba soup
çöpşiş small pieces of meat usually in a kebab

dana eti veal
dil tongue
dil balığı sole
domates tomatoes
domuz eti pork
dondurma ice-cream
döner spit-roast
ekmek bread
elma apple
erik plum
et meat
fasulye beans
fırında oven-roast
hamsi anchovy
havuç carrot
hindi turkey
iç pilav rice stuffing
ıspanak spinach
ıstakoz lobster
istiridye oysters
ızgara grill/grilled
kahve coffee
kalkan balığı turbot
karabiber black pepper
karides shrimps
karışık mixed
kebap kebab
keçi goat
kereviz celery
kestane chestnut
kırmızı biber red pepper

kırmızı şarap red wine
kıyma mince
köfte meat-balls
koyun eti mutton
kuzu eti lamb
lahana cabbage
lahana dolması stuffed cabbage
levrek bass
limon lemon
lokum Turkish delight
maden suyu mineral water
mantar mushroom
midye mussels
mısır sweetcorn
muz banana
omlet omelette
ördek duck
pancar beetroot
patates potatoes
patates kızartması chips
patlıcan aubergine/ eggplant
patlıcan musakkası moussaka
peynir cheese
pide (flat) bread
pilav rice
piliç small chicken
pırasa leek

pirzola cutlet
portakal orange
rakı aniseed spirit
ringa balığı herring
roka rocket
salata salad
salatalık cucumber
şarap wine
sardalya sardines
sarımsak garlic
sebze vegetable
şeftali peach
sığır eti beef
su water
süt milk
tarçın cinnamon
tas kebabı braised lamb
tavada fried
tavşan rabbit
tavuk chicken
tuz salt
tuzsuz without salt
un flour
uskumru mackerel
üzüm grapes
vanilya vanilla
yengeç crab
yeşil zeytin green olives
yoğurt çorbası yoghurt soup
yumurta eggs
zeytin olives

Atlas

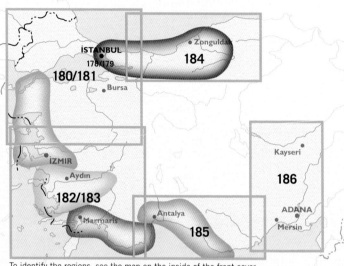

To identify the regions, see the map on the inside of the front cover

Streetplan

▨▨▨ Pedestrian street		▨	Featured place of interest
—·—· Ferry		*i*	Information
▨ Important building			

178/179

0 100 200 300 metres
0 100 200 300 yards

Regional Maps

—·—··— International boundary		o	Village
══════ Major route		▨	Built-up area
▨▨▨▨▨ Motorway		▨	Featured place of interest
───── Main road		■	Place of interest
───── Other road		✈	Airport
□ City			
▫ Major town			
o Town			

180-186

0 10 20 30 40 km
0 5 10 15 20 25 miles

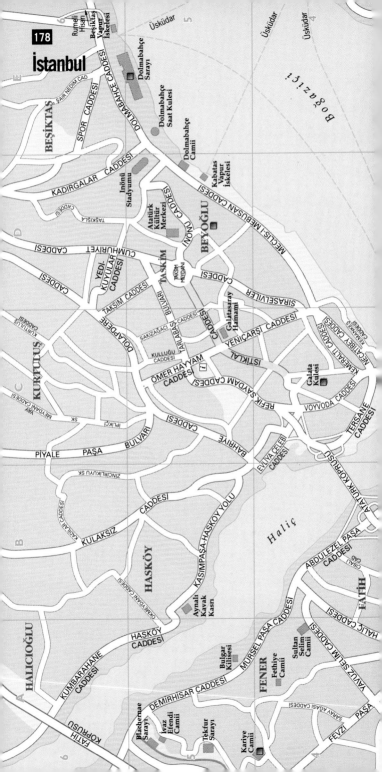

İstanbul

Rumeli Hisarı
Beşiktaş Vapur İskelesi
Üsküdar 5
Üsküdar 4

Dolmabahçe Sarayı

BEŞİKTAŞ

ŞAİR NEDİM CAD

SPOR CADDESİ

DOLMABAHÇE CADDESİ

KADIRGALAR CADDESİ

Dolmabahçe Saat Kulesi

Dolmabahçe Camii

Kabataş Vapur İskelesi

Boğaziçi

İnönü Stadyumu

TAŞKIŞLA CADDESİ

CUMHURİYET CADDESİ

CADDESİ

CADDESİ

YEDİ-KUYULAR CADDESİ

Atatürk Kültür Merkezi

TAKSİM

İNÖNÜ CADDESİ

BEYOĞLU

MECLİSİ MEBUSAN CADDESİ

TAKSİM MEYDANI

TAKSİM CADDESİ

DOLAPDERE CADDESİ

BULVARI

SAKIZAĞACI

TARLABAŞI

KULLUĞU CADDESİ

ÖMER HAYYAM CADDESİ

CADDESİ

CADDESİ

TARLABAŞI CADDESİ

CADDESİ

SIRASELVİLER CADDESİ

Galatasaray Hamamı

YENİÇARŞI CADDESİ

İSTİKLAL CADDESİ

REFİK SAYDAM CADDESİ

i

NECATİBEY CADDESİ

KEMERALTI CADDESİ

KEMANKEŞ CADDESİ

Galata Kulesi

VOYVODA CADDESİ

TERSANE CADDESİ

KURTULUŞ

KURTULUŞ CADDESİ

VAY MEYDANI CADDESİ

SK

İPLİKÇİ

KADİLER CADDESİ

PİYALE PAŞA BULVARI

ZİNCİRLİKUYU SK

BAHRİYE CADDESİ

EVLİYA ÇELEBİ CADDESİ

ATATÜRK KÖPRÜSÜ

Haliç

CADDESİ

KULAKSIZ CADDESİ

KASIMPAŞA-HASKÖY YOLU

OKMEYDANI CADDESİ

HASKÖY

HALICIOĞLU

KUMBARAHANE CADDESİ

FATİH KÖPRÜSÜ

HASKÖY CADDESİ

Aynalı Kavak Kasrı

ABDÜLEZEL PAŞA CADDESİ

CİBALİ CAD

FATİH

HALİÇ CADDESİ

YAVUZ SELİM CADDESİ

MÜRSEL PAŞA CADDESİ

Bulgar Kilisesi

Sultan Selim Camii

FENER

Fethiye Camii

SARAY AĞASI CADDESİ

DEMİRHİSAR CADDESİ

Blachernae Sarayı

İvaz Efendi Camii

Tekfur Sarayı

Kariye Camii

FEVZİ PAŞA

5

4

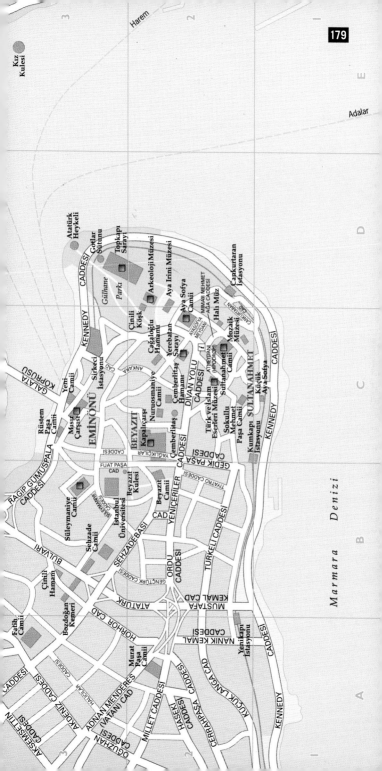

Kız
Kulesi

E

Adalar

D

Harem

Atatürk
Heykeli

Gotlar
Sütunu

Topkapı
Sarayı

Gülhane
Parkı

Arkeoloji Müzesi

Aya İrini Müzesi

CADDESİ

KENNEDY

Çinili
Köşk

Cağaloğlu
Hamamı

Aya Sofya
Camii

Yerebatan
Sarayı

MİMAR MEHMET
AĞA CADDESİ

Mozaik
Müzesi

Hali Müz

CANKURTARAN

Çankurtaran
İstasyonu

GALATA
KÖPRÜSÜ

Sirkeci
İstasyonu

Yeni
Camii

Rüstem
Paşa Camii

Mısır
Çarşısı

EMİNÖNÜ

CAD

ANKARA

Nuruosmaniye
Camii

Çemberlitaş
Hamamı

DİVAN YOLU
CADDESİ

AYASOFYA
MEYDANI

ATMEYDANI
(HİPODROM)

Sultanahmet
Camii

SULTANAHMET

Küçük
Aya Sofya

KENNEDY

CADDESİ

BEYAZIT

Kapalıçarşı

YAĞLIKÇILAR

Çemberlitaş

Türk ve İslam
Eserleri Müzesi

Sokullu
Mehmet
Paşa Camii

Kumkapı
İstasyonu

CADDESİ

Marmara   Denizi

GALATA

RAGİP GUMUSPALA

CADDESİ

Süleymaniye
Camii

FUAT PAŞA
CAD

Beyazıt
Kulesi

İstanbul
Üniversitesi

SÜLEYMANİYE CADDESİ

Beyazıt
Camii

GEDİK PAŞA
CADDESİ

TİYATRO CADDESİ

YENİÇERİLER

CAD

Şehzade
Camii

ŞEHZADEBAŞI

ORDU
CADDESİ

TÜRKELİ CADDESİ

GENÇTÜRK CADDESİ

Çinili
Hamam

BULVARI

Fatih
Camii

Bozdoğan
Kemeri

ATATÜRK CAD

HORHOR CAD

Murat
Paşa Camii

İSTASYON CADDESİ

MİLLET CADDESİ

ADNAN MENDERES
(VATAN) CAD

HASEKİ CADDESİ

CERRAHPAŞA CAD

KÜÇÜK LANGA CAD

CADDESİ

AKDENİZ CADDESİ

OĞUZHAN CADDESİ

HALICILAR

MUSTAFA
KEMAL CAD

NAMIK KEMAL
CADDESİ

Yenikapı
İstasyonu

KENNEDY

AKŞEMSETTİN CADDESİ

B

A

3

2

1

BG

A

B

C

Dereköy

İğneada

E87/555

İstranca

Demirköy

Dağları

Kirklareli

İnece

Sergen

Hasköy

Pınarhisar

Vize

Edirne

Havsa

100

Saray

Babaeski

Lüleburgaz

Beyazköy

Çerkezköy

Kircasalih

E80/0-3

Yarımadası

Ergene Nehri

Çatalca

Ulaş

Çorlu

Uzunköprü

Hayrabolu

Meriç

Muratlı

100

Seymer

Banarlı

GR

Hamidiye

Marmaraereğlisi

E87/550

Tekirdağ

Limanı

Burun

İpsala

Malkara

E84/110

Alexandroúpoli

E84/110

Ballı

Barbaros

Enez

Keşan

Marmara

Adası

Erikli

Şarköy

Marmara

Saros Körfezi

Kara

Burun

Erdek

Bolayır

Karabiga

Bandırma

Gelibolu

Edincik

Gelibolu Yarımadası

E87/550

E90/200

Beliklıçeşme

Kuşcenneti Milliparkı

Gökçeada

Lâpseki

Sinekçi

Kuşçenneti Milliparkı

Kabatepe

Çanakkale Boğazı

Umurbey

Gündoğdu

Biga

Sarıköy

Buğdaylı

Kus

Gölü

Eceabat

Biga

Gelibolu

Çanakkale

Gönen

Milliparkı

Güzelyalı

Çan

Gönen

Manyas

Kirazlı

Kadıköy

Truva

İntepe

Etili

Yenice

Danişment

Bozcaada

Ezine

Küçük

Menderes

Pazarköy

Geyikli

Bayramiç

Kalkım

Balya

Yeniköy

1767m

Kas Dağı

Balıkesir

Ayvacık

Akçay

Gülpınar

Altınoluk

Edremit

230

İvrindi

Ertuğrul

Baba

Assos

Küçükkuyu

Çağış

Burun

Behramkale

Edremit Körfezi

Burhaniye

Madra

Korucu

Alibey

E87/550

565

Adası

Amutova

Savaştepe

GR

Göldük

Ayvalık

Kozak

Sarmısaklı

182

Akrapol

Soma

Gelembe

Altınova

Bergama

Mytilini

Asklepieion

Kırkağaç

Dikili

Pergamum

Lésvos

Çandarlı

Zeytindağ

Akhisar

EGE

DENİZİ

Aliağa

Saruhanlı

Yenifoça

D   E   F

5

184

İğneada
Burun

Kiyiköy

K A R A   D E N İ Z

Karacaköy

Durusu
Gölü

Karaburun

Kumköy
Kilyos

Boğaziçi

Çayağzı

Kefken

Sinekli

Arnavutköy

Kemer-
burgaz

Yeşilvadi

Şile

Ağva

Kandira

Çatalca

Boyalik

Beykoz

Omerli

Teke

Akçaova

Silivri

Büyükçekmece

Yeşilköy

Üsküdar

İSTANBUL

Kartal

Ömerli
Barajı

Kaymaz

Akmeşe

Mollafeneri

Körfez

E80/0-4

İzmit

Sapanca

4

Adalar

100

Gebze

Karamürsel

Gölcük

Derbent

650

**M A R M A R A
D E N İ Z İ**

İmralı
Adası

Çınarcık

Yalova

130

D a ğ l a r ı

Pamukova

Armutlu

S a m a n l ı

Orhangazi

İznik
Gölü

İznik

Osmaneli

Sakarya

3

Gemlik

Mudanya

575

Demirtaş

Yenişehir

Bilecik

Esence

575

Karacabey

E90/200

Hasanağa

BURSA

İnegöl

Pazaryeri

Söğüt

Aksakal

Uluabat
Gölü

2543m
Uludağ

Tahtaköprü

650

565

220

Mustafakemalpaşa

Devecikonağı

Orhaneli

Keles

Domaniç

Bozüyük

E90/200

İnönü

Susurluk

Çuhaçı

Harmancık

650

Kepsut

Dursunbey

Kireç

Gökçedağ

Tavşanlı

Köprüören

Kütahya

555

Bigadiç

A l a ç a m   D a ğ l a r ı

Emet

240

Düvertepe

183

Orencik

Aezanı

Çavdarhisar

650

Simav

Demirci

Eski Gediz

Gediz

Altıntaş

Gördes

Abide

Karabeylı

E96/300

Düzağa

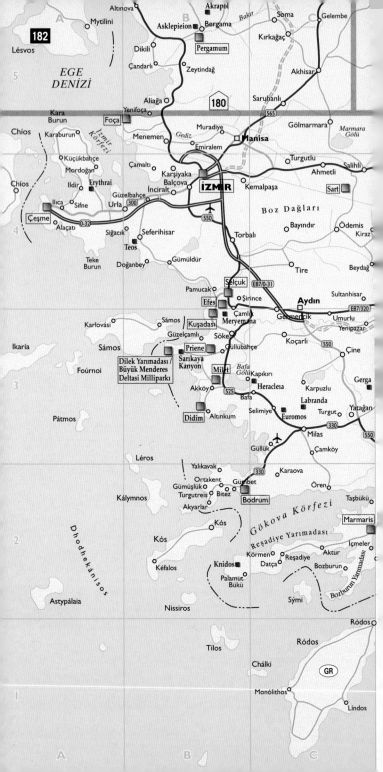

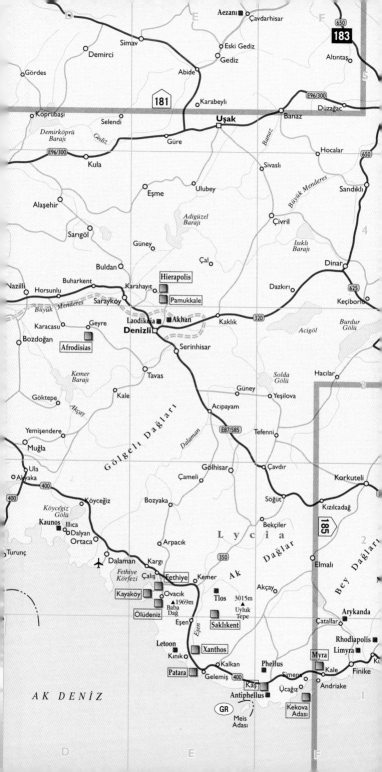

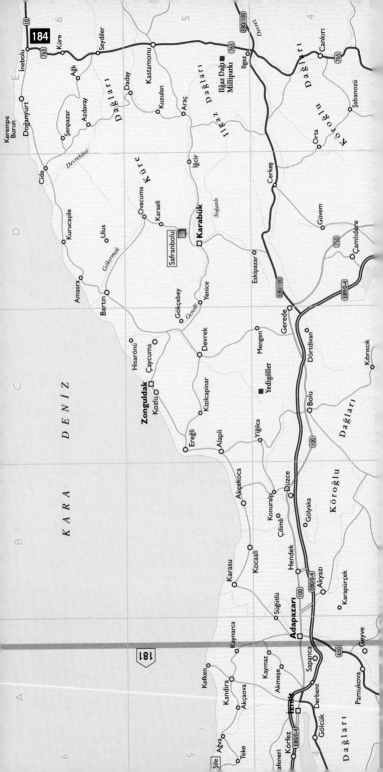

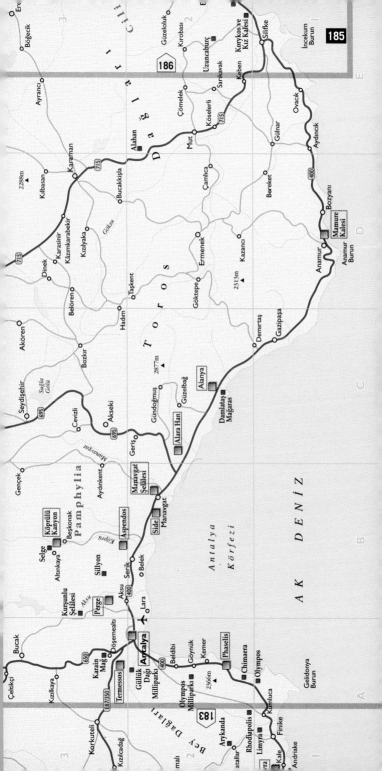

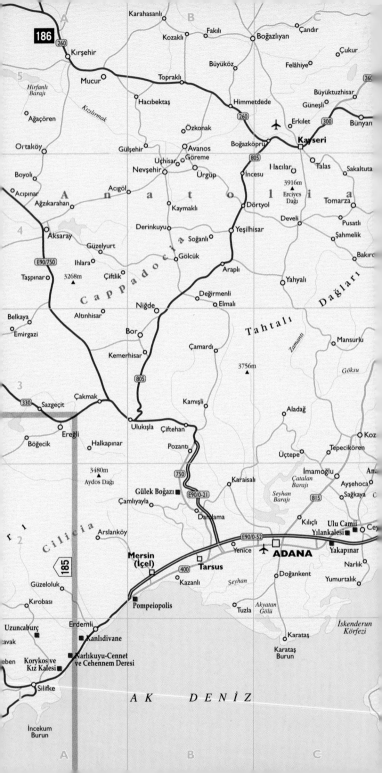

Acknowledgements

The Automobile Association wishes to thank the following photographers and libraries for their assistance in the preparation of this book.

Front and back cover; (t) AA PHOTO LIBRARY/TONY SOUTER, (ct) AA PHOTO LIBRARY/JEANFRANÇOIS PIN, (cb) AA PHOTO LIBRARY/PAUL KENWARD, (b) AA PHOTO LIBRARY/JEAN FRANÇOIS PIN, Spine AA PHOTO LIBRARY/PAUL KENWARD.

ALLSPORT UK LTD 22/3; HEATHER ANGEL 25t; BRUCE COLEMAN COLLECTION 24l; MARY EVANS PICTURE LIBRARY 16/17b/gr, 16b, 17t, 17c; HULTON ARCHIVE 14t; PICTURES COLOUR LIBRARY 2(i), 5; TURGAY TUNA 23; WORLD PICTURES 24r.

The remaining photographs are held in the Association's own library (AA PHOTO LIBRARY) and were taken by PETE BENNETT, with the exception of the following: PAUL KENWARD 6/7, 39t, 55, 56, 63, 97, 138/9, 173r; DARIO MITIDERI 15t, 15c, 20/1, 99; JEAN FRANÇOIS PIN 12t, 17b, 26, 62b, 72, 81t, 82, 120; CLIVE SAWYER 40, 48, 81b; TONY SOUTER 9b, 21, 43.

Lindsay Bennett wishes to thank Dogan Beylar and Christina Frohly for their invaluable help and assistance during research for this book, along with the staff of the Dalyan Cooperative for their practical help.
Kevin Gould wishes to thank Munir Akdogan for his invaluable help during the research for this book.

Questionnaire

Dear Traveller
Your comments, opinions and recommendations are very important to us. Please help us to improve our travel guides by taking a few minutes to complete this simple questionnaire.

You do not need a stamp (unless posted outside the UK). If you do not want to remove this page from your guide, then photocopy it or write your answers on a plain sheet of paper.

Send to: The Editor, Spiral Guides, AA World Travel Guides, FREEPOST SCE 4598, Basingstoke RG21 4GY.

Your recommendations...
We always encourage readers' recommendations for restaurants, night-life or shopping – if your recommendation is used in the next edition of the guide, we will send you a FREE AA Spiral Guide of your choice. Please state below the establishment name, location and your reasons for recommending it.

_____

_____

_____

_____

_____

Please send me AA Spiral _____
(see list of titles inside the back cover)

About this guide...
Which title did you buy?

_____ **AA Spiral**

Where did you buy it? _____

When? m m / y y

Why did you choose an AA Spiral Guide? _____

_____

_____

_____

_____

Did this guide meet your expectations?

Exceeded ☐ Met all ☐ Met most ☐ Fell below ☐

Please give your reasons _____

_____

_____

_____

_____

continued on next page...

Were there any aspects of this guide that you particularly liked?

_____
_____
_____
_____
_____

Is there anything we could have done better?

_____
_____
_____
_____

About you...

Name (Mr/Mrs/Ms) _____

Address _____

_____ **Postcode** _____

Daytime tel no _____ **email** _____

Please _only_ give us your email address and mobile phone number if you wish to hear from us about other products and services from the AA and partners by email or text or mms.

Which age group are you in?

Under 25 ☐   25–34 ☐   35–44 ☐   45–54 ☐   55–64 ☐   65+ ☐

How many trips do you make a year?

Less than one ☐   One ☐   Two ☐   Three or more ☐

Are you an AA member? Yes ☐   **No** ☐

About your trip...

When did you book? mm / y y   **When did you travel?** mm / y y

How long did you stay? _____

Was it for business or leisure? _____

Did you buy any other travel guides for your trip? ☐ Yes   ☐ No

If yes, which ones? _____

Thank you for taking the time to complete this questionnaire. Please send it to us as soon as possible, and remember, you do not need a stamp (unless posted outside the UK).